D1242637

DISCARD

Emeril Lagasse

Emeril Lagasse

Don Rauf

Enslow Publishing

101 W. 23rd Street
Suite 240
New York, NY 10011
USA

enslow.com

Published in 2016 by Enslow Publishing, LLC
101 W. 23rd Street, Suite 240, New York, NY 10011

Library of Congress Cataloging-in-Publication Data

Rauf, Don, author.
    Emeril Lagasse / Don Rauf
        pages cm. — (Celebrity chefs)
    Includes bibliographical references and index.
    Summary: "Describes the life and career of chef Emeril Lagasse"—
Provided by publisher.
    ISBN 978-0-7660-7197-1
    1. Lagasse, Emeril—Juvenile literature. 2. Celebrity chefs—United States—
Biography—Juvenile literature. I. Title.
    TX649.L34R38 2016
    641.5092—dc23
    [B]
                            2015026891

Printed in the United States of America

To Our Readers: We have done our best to make sure all website addresses in this book were active and appropriate when we went to press. However, the author and the publisher have no control over and assume no liability for the material available on those websites or on any websites they may link to. Any comments or suggestions can be sent by e-mail to customerservice@enslow.com.

CONTENTS

★

With his warm personality and high energy, Emeril Lagasse has inspired generations of novice cooks to have fun in the kitchen.

Chapter

1

A Chef
at an Early Age

"Bam!" That's the catchphrase of one of the most famous chefs in America, and it really captures how Emeril Lagasse's life has been right from the beginning. Lagasse didn't have a gentle rise to success in the cooking world. He came out of the gate, charging full-speed ahead with his own forceful "Bam!" Working hard at a very young age, he became one of the top culinary artists in the country when he was only in his twenties. His achievements came in leaps and bounds, and that's the same energy he brought to his popular cooking show, *Emeril Live.*

That program made him famous throughout the country and around the world. For years, he gained millions of fans and showed a generation of women, men—and even kids—that they could cook. Today, he is still a popular celebrity chef and the leader of a multimillion-dollar Creole cuisine empire that includes cookbooks, food-related products, and television shows. How did he get to the top of the culinary world? It took a lot of dedication and hard work. "Life just doesn't hand you things," Lagasse once said. "You have to get out there and make things happen...that's the exciting part."[1] And Emeril has truly lived by those words.

A Family of Food Lovers

Born October 15, 1959, in Fall River, Massachusetts, Emeril Lagasse got both his strong work ethic and his love of cooking from his Portuguese mother, Hilda, and his French Canadian father, who was also named Emeril but went by John or "Mr. John" for those who knew him closely. The middle child of three, Emeril has an older sister, Delores, and a younger brother, Mark.

His father really showed Emeril the value and importance of hard work. When Emeril's father was a 12-year-old boy, he had to quit school to work on the farm and help support the family. When John was providing for his family as an adult, he toiled away dyeing suit linings at Duro Finishing, a local textile mill. He often worked the second shift and put in thirty-five years there before retiring. He also moonlighted as a security guard and as a cab driver to help pay the family bills. In an in interview in *Cigar Aficionado* magazine, Lagasse said, "[My father's] not a talker. He's a very shy, quiet guy, but he has tremendous respect for people and tremendous respect for the work ethic. You can cry all you want that life is hard. The only way you're going to

> *"Life just doesn't hand you things. You have to get out there and make things happen . . . that's the exciting part."*—Emeril

Lagasse grew up in Fall River, Massachusetts, a blue-collar Portuguese-American community. Fall River was home to many textile factories in the nineteenth century. Emeril learned the value of hard work from his father, and he inherited his love of food from his mother.

get ahead is to push and work hard. If you do it from your heart and don't screw anybody over along the way, eventually you're going to get ahead, because it all comes back to you."[2]

In the Lagasse family, so much of life revolved around food, eating, and the kitchen. Because his mother was a very good and enthusiastic home chef, Emeril got very involved preparing food. As young as five years old, he was at his mother's side as she made soup. The child chef would help put the vegetables into the pot. His mother noticed that he had a natural ability in the kitchen. Once he got in front of the oven and counters, he wanted to take over. Sometimes his mother could not get to the stove because he would be in the way. As he got older, he helped more and more in the kitchen. He has said that his mother was a great teacher, and it was his mother that showed him that food was a great way to make people happy.

Emeril didn't grow up with just that standard American food or TV dinners like many of his friends. His mother's Portuguese-influenced food had strong, exotic flavors. She loved spicy piri piri sauce that often combines cayenne, garlic, paprika and chili flakes, and goes very well with chicken. His mother also made a Portuguese kale soup when Emeril was growing up. Called Caldo Verde because of its green color, the soup was often served on Portuguese feast days in the Lagasse household.

Although his father didn't cook as much, he was no slouch in the kitchen. Almost every Sunday, Mr. John would put on the apron and prepare *linguiça,* a long, dry Portuguese sausage made with coarsely chopped pork, garlic and paprika. His father and his uncle also owned a farm, so from a young age, Emeril always had a sense of what it was like to have fresh produce.

Another "Grandmother" and a Source of Inspiration

Emeril's mother had a great friend, Ines De Costa, a woman who owned a local restaurant, the St. John's Athletic Club. Emeril and his mother would visit Ines and see what she was cooking up in the kitchen.

Ines loved to feed and nourish people. For Emeril, Ines was like a close family member and he called her "vo," which in Portuguese means grandmother. Emeril was so curious in Ines's kitchen that she would often scold him for fiddling with her ingredients.

Emeril was totally inspired by Ines's work ethic and her recipes; he has included many of her recipes in his cookbooks. One was her version of kale soup featuring red and white beans. Years later, she called Emeril to tell him he was using too much salt in her recipe.

Emeril is very close with his mother, Hilda Lagasse. In fact, he credits Hilda with introducing him to cooking. From Hilda's home kitchen, Emeril moved on to work in a bakery at the tender age of ten.

Like most young boys, Emeril did have other interests besides food. He delivered newspapers. He practiced karate. He played baseball and he feverishly followed his favorite team, the Boston Red Sox. (He has remained a Boston Red Sox fan his whole life). He joined the Cub Scouts. He was also known as the class clown at school. He had a natural ability to make people laugh. Classmates have said that he put people at ease.

The Boy Baker

At age 10, he was ready to earn cash and he somehow convinced the owners of Carreiro's bakery to hire him as a dishwasher. The Portuguese bakers knew him well because his mother always sent him to the bakery to fetch bread for the family. After school for four hours each day, he would wash the pans and earn one dollar per hour. He proved himself to be a reliable worker and after a couple years, the bakery promoted him.

Emeril was gradually given work handling the baking of items. He started with muffins. When he proved himself with muffins, Emeril worked up the baking ladder. He mastered sweet breads, custards, cornbreads, and Portuguese pastries. In his cookbook *Emeril's New New Orleans Cookbook*, he writes, "I was thrilled by the concept that using a foolproof formula, I could create perfect cakes, breads and pastries."[3] Emeril has fond memories of sitting around the stainless steel flour bins and talking with the Portuguese men who worked there. Just as he saw food to be a source of joy at home for his family, Emeril saw how baked goods also made customers happy.

His baking started to wreak havoc on his school schedule. Baking was generally an activity that had to be done at night so the bakery could have fresh baked goods ready for the morning. Emeril's parents appreciated his passion for cooking, so they let the budding chef follow a crazy schedule. Emeril would arrive at the bakery at 11 p.m. and work all the way until morning when it was time to go to school. He'd make it through his classes and then rush home. His mother would feed him at 3 p.m., and he would go straight to sleep. Some time along the way he would find time to do his homework. His parents told him he had to keep up a B-plus average to work this crazy schedule, and somehow he managed it.

Eventually, he wanted to learn more, so he got time off to take a continuing education class in cake decorating at night. He perfected butter cream frostings and made beautiful icing flowers. He got so good at making cakes and cake decoration that he won a class competition and went on to win a bigger regional competition to make wedding cakes.

He Also Had the Music in Him

Working long hours at cooking was not much of a hardship for Emeril because he loved cooking so much. He also had a passion for music and loved to play drums. By age eight, he was playing in a huge local Portuguese band that had forty-five members. For a while, he even toured around New England and Canada. He joined other bands as well. At one point, he was drumming in a dance band called the Royal Aces playing the hits at weddings, dances, parties, and religious festivals. He even led the high school drum squad and he once played in a backup band for the rock group Aerosmith. He was an ever curious learner. He didn't just learn the drums, he taught himself to play trombone, flute, and trumpet.

While part of him was drawn to following a musical path, food had a bigger pull. His high school offered a vocational training program in the culinary arts, at nearby Diman Regional

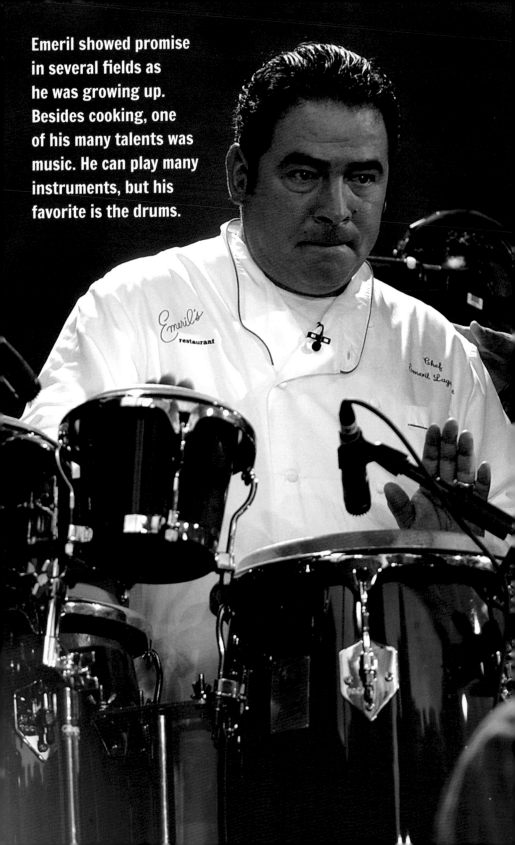

Emeril showed promise in several fields as he was growing up. Besides cooking, one of his many talents was music. He can play many instruments, but his favorite is the drums.

Because he knew from an early age that he wanted to cook, Emeril was able to get a head start. The boy who had started working in food services at ten went on to study culinary arts at a special high school.

Vocational High School, so the fourteen-year-old Emeril pursued that course. His teachers there remember Emeril as an incredibly hard worker, full of energy, who wanted to perfect his techniques and get things done. He seemed to have an endless curiosity and need to learn new things. One of his teachers remembered him as a strong leader as well.

Emeril kept up with his music while he honed his cooking chops, and he became a very skilled player. He got so good that the New England Conservatory offered him a scholarship to attend the school. Now Emeril was at a difficult crossroads. He recognized what a tremendous offer it was to receive a scholarship, but he was torn. After he gave it careful thought, he decided his true path lay with cooking and he'd have to leave music on a back burner.

His decision was not an immediate hit with his parents. His mother was especially upset. Emeril remembers her chasing him around the neighborhood a few times. She didn't think cooking was going to pay off. Emeril has said that he understood his mother's point of view because in the 1970s, being a guy who cooked was not something that many men aspired to. His father was more supportive. Mr. John wasn't working in a job that was his true passion. He told his son that if this was something he truly loved, he should go for it. A lot of Emeril's friends wound up working in the same plant where his father worked, and his father wanted him to have more than that.

Full Speed
Ahead

In 1977, Lagasse decided to pay his own way through the culinary program at Johnson & Wales College of Culinary Arts in Providence, Rhode Island. To pay for school, he worked nights at an Italian restaurant called Venus de Milo, located close by in Swansee, Massachusetts. Here, Lagasse slaved away peeling onions and potatoes, but his hard work paid off when he was promoted to chef de cuisine. He also met his first wife here. He and Elizabeth Kief were married just a few months after he completed his studies at Johnson & Wales in 1978. (The school would later go on to award him an honorary doctorate degree.)

In an interview in The *Orlando Sentinel*, Emeril said, "I commuted, lived at home, went to school and worked seventy hours a week to pay for school and a car and all that kind of stuff," he said. "The one thing that my mom and dad instilled in me, besides an unbelievable work ethic, is that there's no free ride in life."[1]

Friends who knew him in cooking school said that he was serious about his studies, but he was always a tinkerer. He looked at recipes and thought how he could improve them

Emeril continued his culinary
education at Johnson & Wales in 1977.
The prestigious culinary university
now celebrates its famous alumnus
in a museum exhibit on campus.

or put his own spin on them. He tried different spices, different amounts of ingredients, and different combinations. Sometimes he'd add more ingredients; sometimes he would subtract them. Experimenting was important to find the dishes and flavors that would define who he was as a chef.

The European Seal of Approval

After two years getting down the techniques of a restaurant chef, Lagasse secured employment with the Sheraton Hotel in Philadelphia, working in its kitchen. He next wanted work in New York City, but he soon found out that he was not fully equipped to compete in that culinary world. At the time, in the mid-1970s, New York restaurants were interested in European cuisine. French, German and Swiss chefs ran the kitchens. Lagasse felt he needed to get more training in the fine art of classic French cuisine if he were to progress with his career. Having experience in European kitchens could help open doors back in the United States.

> *"The one thing that my mom and dad instilled in me, besides an unbelievable work ethic, is that there's no free ride in life."*

So, Lagasse packed his knives and took off to Paris and Lyon in France, where he refined his skills as a chef by apprenticing in restaurants there. Lagasse has said that his training in Europe was tougher than he expected. Even though he had a two-year degree in the culinary arts, European chefs gave his American degree little regard, according to Emeril. He said that European chefs thought that all American chefs could prepare were hamburgers, hot dogs, and french fries. These chefs yelled at him, laughed at him, and treated him poorly overall. He was often pushed to do the grunt work. He also said that he faced some bias from chefs who learned he was part Portuguese. Portuguese workers were often the dishwashers in fine European dining establishments. Chefs would tell him that he was lucky to be cooking at all because of his Portuguese background. Despite the hard time, Lagasse said he learned from the experience. His biggest lesson: It doesn't matter where you're from, if you find what you love to do you have to follow your passion. "I mean, if you love what you do—whether you're an auto mechanic or you sew clothes or you cook—it's all about personal passion and love that really makes the thrust to [take you to] the level that you want to get it to," Lagasse said.[2]

After weathering the rigorous conditions in French eateries and absorbing all he could, Lagasse returned to the U.S. with another selling point on his resume. The time spent in France helped open doors. When he came back to the states, he landed a job with the famous chef Wolfgang Puck in New York City at the Berkshire Place Hotel. Puck was one of the most famous chefs in the world at the time. Under his savvy guidance, Lagasse entered the high-pressure world of working as a line chef preparing Puck's versions of nouvelle cuisine—an eclectic style of preparing French food.

Lagasse soon moved on to work as a sous chef at the Parker House (also called Parker's Restaurant) in Boston. The restaurant is one of the oldest in the country, and it has been known for fine dining since the late 1800s. The Parker House gained legendary status as the venue that invented the Boston Cream Pie, which is really a cake filled with custard and covered in

Five Things Emeril
★ **Cannot Live Without**

In *Restaurant Hospitality* magazine, in April 2015, Emeril listed the five things he could not live without.[3]

1. Celery salt. I use it in almost everything. People don't usually guess that it's in there, but I can tell you that it adds oomph to many dishes. My test kitchen team was very surprised when I shared this secret with them.

2. Electric deep fryer. It helps me fry things at the proper temperature, and that's the most important part of frying. Fry right or don't fry at all.

3. Instant-read thermometer. It takes the guess-work out of cooking meats to the perfect temperature.

4. *The Way to Cook*. I don't often need to pull out a cookbook, because at home I cook very simply for my family, but when I do need a reference for something, I take a look at Julia Child's *The Way to Cook*. Her recipes never disappoint and are so well written.

5. Immersion blender. I was so happy when immersion blenders came on the market. In my restaurants they are indispensable. At home, if you're making a smooth soup or puree, they come in handy and are a real time-saver, too.

Emeril was talented enough to land a job working at one of Wolfgang Puck's restaurants in New York City. The Austrian chef was taking the US restaurant scene by storm, revolutionizing food and creating a popular brand.

The Parker House is a Boston institution. Not only has its restaurant served presidents and dignitaries, but its kitchen has been home to many talented and influential chefs. Emeril learned the art of cooking for the fine dining experience at the Parker House.

chocolate. The restaurant was not only a training ground for Emeril, but for chefs Lydia Shire and Jasper White—both famous Boston-based chefs and restaurateurs. Even Malcom X worked there as a busboy in the 1940s. At Parker House, Emeril learned to make Boston scrod and the Parker House rolls, which have become a staple at many other restaurants. For example, chef Tom Collicchio, who hosts the TV show *Top Chef*, serves Parker House rolls at his New York City restaurant Collicchio and Sons. Parker House really gave Emeril a broad view of what it is like to work in a fine dining establishment.

The Continual Learner

As the dedicated chef that he was, Emeril would use his time off productively to learn more. While at Parker House, he began keeping a wine notebook. Whenever he had a night off, he would buy a $10 bottle of wine and spend time savoring it, studying it, and taking notes. He would jot down how it tasted and smelled. His own self-teaching method gave him a great appreciation of wine that he has carried with him throughout his life.

He also wanted to learn what other top chefs of his time were up to. He took a trip to Alice Waters's Chez Panisse in Berkeley, California. Chef Waters was known as one of the pioneers of a style of cooking called California cuisine, and she promoted the idea of sourcing foods locally. Waters used products from dairies, ranchers, and farms near to her restaurant. Lagasse also took inspiration from eating at Larry Forgione's An American Place in New York City. Forgione has been called the Godfather of American Cuisine. Like Waters, Forgione was also part of what was called the farm-to-table movement, using only products that were in season and from local farms at his critically-acclaimed restaurant. Lagasse kept notes on all the

★ Emeril's Daughters

Now in their 30s, Jillian and Jessie Lagasse are both following the footsteps of their father. While they are not working as professional chefs, they have teamed up to publish two cookbooks—*The Gluten Free Table* and *The Lagasse Girls' Big Flavor, Bold Taste and No Gluten*. Neither of his daughters can eat gluten. Jessie has a gluten intolerance and Jillian has celiac disease. Celiac disease is a condition that creates inflammation in the small intestine and damage in the lining.

Like their father, Emeril's daughters, Jessie Lagasse Swanson (left) and Jillian Lagasse, have a passion for cooking. Their two cookbooks feature gluten-free recipes.

eateries he visited, making sure to remember the elements that worked and those that did not.

Making His Mark in New England

The next stop for Emeril was the Dunfey Hotels in Maine and Cape Cod. Here, he worked as sous chef and director of food and beverage. He was soon promoted and worked as an executive chef in South Portland, Maine, at a restaurant called Seasons. One of his old managers, Fern Genest, remembered Lagasse as somewhat quiet but with a sense of humor: "He was very low key, very serious about cooking, but fun—he liked to joke around. The staff loved him."[4]

Genest said that Lagasse came up with an idea to take color photographs of the dishes served at Seasons so that the cooks could match their dishes to look like the ones in the photos. If the meals didn't look like the pictures, they had to be done again. Genest thought that Emeril didn't take very well to corporate control, but that was part of the structure at Seasons. He had to get all his ideas approved first through specific food-and-beverage guidelines set up by management, but he didn't like going through that bureaucratic process.

In Portland, he and his wife Elizabeth began to raise a family. They had a baby girl, Jessica, and Emeril would spend some time with her, but he was putting in very long hours in the kitchen, so family time was limited.

By 1979 at age twenty, he had been promoted to executive chef at Dunfey's Hyannis Resort in Cape Cod, Massachusetts. Reports from that time said that the restaurant was bleeding money. When Lagasse stepped in, the young chef tightened operations and turned the kitchen around so it was running efficiently and within budget. His efforts stopped the eatery from losing any more money.

Through and through, from his accent to his style of cooking, Emeril was now defining himself as a New England chef. Anyone looking at his career path in these early days would think the he might one day become one of the best chefs in this region. Fate, however, was going to take an interesting turn and send Emeril in a totally new and transforming direction.

Chapter 3

A Song of
the South

C ommander's Palace is a legendary restaurant in New Orleans, Louisiana. The restaurant opened in 1880 in a tree-lined area of the city known as the Garden District. Since then, the restaurant has been a fine dining establishment known for its "Old World" charm and gentility. With its white linens, the restaurant provides a proper dining atmosphere and it insists that diners dress accordingly. Men are urged to wear jackets. Collared shirts and closed-toe shoes are a must. If you come in shorts, flip-flops, t-shirts, sweat shirts, or sweat pants, you won't get in. Jeans are frowned upon. Commander's Palace continues to be one of the most famous and critically acclaimed restaurants in the country.

The crowds pack in for the restaurant's haute Cajun and Creole cuisine. Blending French, West African, Amerindian, Spanish, Portuguese, and Caribbean influences, Creole is a style of cooking that originated with the local people of Louisiana. Cajun is also another closely related style of local cuisine, but it comes from early French settlers who originated in Canada

After working at several restaurants in New England, Emeril set his sights on New Orleans, where good food is as important as a friendly attitude. Commander's Palace is one of the city's oldest and most respected restaurants, and its owners wanted Emeril to run their kitchen.

and made their way to the far south in America. Over time, the Cajun and Creole cultures have overlapped in many ways, and they share many of the same spices and flavors. Still, some think of Creole as "city food" and Cajun as "country food." Creole is related to more refined European-style cooking, while Cajun is generally a spicier, rustic style of preparing food. Some food experts say that Creole cuisine uses tomatoes and proper Cajun food does not.

Over the years, Commander's Palace has delighted diners with its versions of New Orleans classics— shrimp remoulade (rom-oo-lawd), seafood gumbo, oysters Rockefeller, trout amandine (featuring slivered almonds), and pompano en papillotte (a fish cooked in sealed parchment paper).

The Grand Dame Needs a Star

In 1982, the venerable Commander's Palace was in desperate need of a hot chef to maintain the classic dishes, recharge the place with new energy, and boost the profile of the restaurant on a national scale. At this time, a headhunter who specialized in finding restaurants new, fresh talent happened to be traveling through Cape Cod. He had dinner at Emeril Lagasse's restaurant and was highly impressed. The twenty-three-year-old Lagasse was churning out some exciting, top-notch New England-style chow.

The headhunter contacted Ella and Dick Brennan, the owners of Commander's Palace, to tell them about his find. They asked about Lagasse's résumé and the headhunter told them that they didn't need to see one. He told them to trust him—this guy could really cook. Based on the headhunter's rave, Ella Brennan decided to give Lagasse a call. It was the first of a long series of conversations. Ella wanted to make sure they were hiring the right chef, so she didn't rush to bring Lagasse on board. All told, the job interview process took about four months. It may have been one of the longest job interviews in history.

In an interview in *Cigar Aficionado*, Lagasse recalled, "Every week we would talk. She would say, 'Today, I want to talk about what inspires you. Is bread inspiring you? Is a book inspiring you?' Ella is a genius with people. We would talk for a half hour, forty minutes. The next Wednesday, the phone would ring: 'Today, I want to talk about your philosophies about people. How do you motivate people?'"[1] One call was all about wine. Another was about what he had been cooking all week. And so the process went, and Lagasse went along with it.

After interviewing him three times in one week, Ella told him that he now had to come down to New Orleans in person—and it couldn't be just for a short weekend. A day or two would not do. She told him that she needed him to give a Thursday, Friday, Saturday, Sunday, and Monday. Plus, Ella's family was big and she wanted him to meet the whole family. Lagasse made arrangement for his work to be covered in New England and he booked a flight south.

A First Taste of New Orleans

For Lagasse, the trip did not start very well. The plane ride was horrible and the airline lost his luggage. After a long cab ride, he finally got to Commander's Palace at about 9:30 p.m. He was feeling a bit frazzled and burnt out from the travel, but he was immediately taken by the warm glow of Commander's Place. When he met Ella, she was graciously ushering some diners to the door to say goodnight. Lagasse told her of his rough ride down and his lost luggage. Ella turned immediately to the maître d' and asked him to fetch Emeril a toothbrush. She then told him that they were going to go to the bar and have a drink. It was time to get acquainted.

As the nervous Emeril and poised Ella walked through the kitchen to the bar, she asked him what he thought of the place so far. He said, "Smells just like my mom's kitchen."[2] Looking back, Ella has said that Emeril pretty much sealed the deal with those words, but she wasn't going to tell him until the long-weekend visit was over.

They toured all parts of the city that long weekend and met with the large Brennan family. At some point during Sunday dinner, Ella's brother Dick left the table after fifteen or twenty minutes. Soon, Ella was told she had a phone call. She picked up the phone and was surprised to hear her brother on the other end. He wanted to get her alone to tell her that he thought Lagasse was that man they needed for the job.

By the end of the visit, Ella was impressed by Lagasse's integrity, enthusiasm, cooking skill, and energy. He got the job. This young chef, just in his twenties, was now executive chef at one of the most famous restaurants in America.

For Emeril Lagasse, this was the beginning of a trans-forming experience. The New England chef now had to win over Louisiana diners. How could this Northerner possibly master Southern cuisine? Luckily, he had the best support he could hope for in Ella Brennan. Emeril had liked Ella instantly. He held her in high regard, and their professional relationship and mutual admiration grew strong over the years as he mastered the dishes of Commander's Palace. He has called Ella his second mother.

Although she didn't know much at all about how to cook, Ella Brennan had a keen sense of what went into making fantastic, memorable meals. Sometimes, she would go through a new cookbook and flag the dishes that sounded good. She would then hand the book over to Lagasse and tell him that some of the dishes may be a bit too fancy, but they sounded terrific. She asked him to "Creolize" them and make them into great New Orleans dishes. Both Ella and Dick had high standards and Emeril has said that the Brennans pushed him to cook better and work harder.

Taming a Terrible Temper

Lagasse has given Ella a lot of credit for shaping him into the chef he is today. She even adjusted his temperament. In Europe, he saw that some of the best chefs operate by yelling when things were not as they should be. Ella saw that Lagasse would often "fly off the handle" and get very mad, even at small things. She counseled him to dial his temper down a few notches. She helped him develop a warmer, calmer management style. He got better at dealing with people and resolving problems in a less explosive manner.

Lagasse has admitted that he was "harsh" when he first started. Ella made him realize that he didn't need to be rude to people. Every now and then when Ella saw him be unreasonable with his temper, she would take he yellow legal pad and scrawl a note for him like "When you wake up tomorrow, leave your ego at home." She'd tear off the notes and silently hand them to Emeril. He'd often be a little taken aback at first, but her note system had its intended effect.[3]

"If you respect people and treat them the way you want to be treated and do it with intelligence and finesse, you could walk into the room wearing a T-shirt and they'll know you're the chef," Emeril has said about his development as a chef.

Ella Brennan hired Emeril to run her famed restaurant. But first she put the young chef through his paces, and she counseled him to tame his hot-headed personality. Emeril has called Brennan his second mother, and he credits her with his maturation as a chef and as a man.

"I have my sessions where I have to get my point across, but I never do it in public anymore. It's always closed-door. I'll take them [employees] for a ride in my car, buy them a cup of coffee, or have them over to my house. I've calmed way, way down."[4]

Along the way, however, Emeril has dramatically blown his stack. When a fish salesman tried to sell him inferior seafood, he got so furious that he heaved all the fish out onto the sidewalk. Once a customer insisted that the fish he was eating was not salmon. When Emeril was told this, he stormed into the dining room holding the entire salmon in his hand. He put it in front of the customer's face and asked him to explain how the fish he was holding was not a salmon.

Emeril attributes these temper flare-ups to having high standards. He always wants to give the best quality. He wants to honor the traditions. If things are sub par, then he loses control and gets upset. He won't suffer for inferior product. Emeril has always expected his employees to give their all and give their best. And in return he has recognized their efforts.

Ti Martine worked as a cook at Commander's Palace under Emeril. One of her very first tasks was to take a tray of 100 live soft-shell crabs and pull their eyes out. She knew Emeril was testing her, and she passed with flying colors. She also said that Emeril was constantly running all over the kitchen saying to the cooks, "Did you taste it? Taste it again."[5]

Finding His New Orleans Voice

It wasn't just Ella and the Brennan family that made him jump aboard Commander's Palace. He also fell in love with New Orleans, nicknamed the Big Easy. He loved the culture and the music, and how the people there seemed enjoy both so much. Although he didn't know it at the time, over the years to come

Pictured here are many of the best and brightest chefs to work at Commander's Palace. To Emeril Lagasse's right stands Chef Paul Prudhomme, Emeril's predecessor. Prudhomme is credited with turning Commander's Palace from a good restaurant into a world-class dining destination.

the New England boy would come to represent the city and be a symbol of New Orleans.

When he slipped into the executive chef apron at Commander's Palace, he had to do two things when it came to the menu. He had to maintain the classics but also update the menu and bring his own touch to preparing the food there. Commander's Palace had many fans and the institution expected certain dishes on the menu and a certain style of cooking. In his book *Emeril's New New Orleans Cooking,* Emeril has described old New Orleans food as delicious but heavy. He lists the following as traditional favorites: baked, smothered oysters; shrimp remoulade, crabmeat ravigote (featuring a highly seasoned sauce of white wine, vinegar, butter, cream, and mushrooms), stuffed artichokes, and a thickly rouxed gumbo. (Roux, pronounced "roo" is a thickening agent made of butter or fat and flour.)

So the Louisiana Seafood Court-Bouillon stuffed with shrimp stayed. So did the oysters in a Cajun sauce. Some dishes were new—pecan-crusted gulf fish, muscadine and chicory coffee-lacquered quail, and grilled veal chop. Bread pudding soufflé was still on the menu but it was joined by lemon flan, coffee fudge sheba and a cheese plate. Emeril tweaked and modified. He brought in some spices and methods from his upbringing with Portuguese cooking. And New Orleans brought its influences to Emeril. As Ella said, "We Creolized him."[6]

Emeril needed to show that he was taking charge. Soon after he started, he threw away the canned goods—he wanted everything to be fresh and made from scratch— from ice cream to Worcestershire sauce. He canceled many of the old contracts that the kitchen had with food sellers, and he reached out to local growers and seafood providers that he thought were providing the highest quality. When he first arrived in Louisiana, he

The History of
★ Louisiana Cuisine

In 1682, the explorer Robert La Salle claimed Louisiana for France. In 1718, another French explorer named Jean-Baptiste Le Moyne, Sieur de Bienville founded what is now New Orleans, and a great influx of French colonists arrived and settled in the area. Even then the French were known for their love of food, but they did not have the ingredients or spices from their mother country. They combined their French cooking approaches with Native ingredients and Indian spices. The blending of cultures and cuisines in the Louisiana area became known a Creole. At first, Creole simply referred to the French and Spanish colonists. But Creole took on different meanings over time. Some used the term to refer to the French-speaking blacks of the area. Creole also refers to a language that developed in the region that combines French with some influences of Portuguese, Spanish, local Indian, and West African languages.

In the mid 1700s, the French in Canada who refused to swear allegiance to England were deported. Many wound up in the area of Louisiana. In Canada, these people of French descent were known as Acadians. In New Orleans, their name became Cajun. The Cajuns developed different kinds of spicy stews such as gumbo and jambalaya. The Cajuns tended to favor cooking meals all in one pot. Their food was more of country cooking, with pungent and peppery flavors. Their ingredients would often feature duck, frog, pork, sausage, beans, yams, and pecans. Creole, on the other hand, was more refined and delicate. They had picked up aristocratic influences from the French and Spanish. Oysters Rockefeller is considered a dish that represents a Creole sensibility. These are raw oysters served with finely minced spinach, onion, parsley and breadcrumbs. Over the years, many of the styles of the two cuisines have intermingled.

thought it was nothing more than a soggy water-filled swamp. But as he started to search for the freshest and best ingredients he discovered the bounty that Louisiana had to offer.

He visited strawberry fields, butcher shops, and fishing ports. By driving around the state, he discovered the great web of waterways teeming with blue crabs, sweet shrimp, plump oysters, and succulent crawfish. Along the country roads, he saw the fields of sugarcane, rice, and sweet potatoes, and the pecan and peach orchards. The roadside gardens sold okra, bell peppers, tomatoes, and eggplant. He visited the McIllhenny Co. on Avery Island. The company has built a worldwide reputation for raising hot peppers and making Tabasco sauce. At the butcher shops, Emeril found the meats to be different from New England. Here he could buy andouille (a spicy smoked sausage), boudin (a sausage made of rice, pork, onions, green peppers, and seasonings), and grattons (bite-sized, deep-fried cubes of pig fat).

Lagasse developed ideas of the types of dishes he wanted to prepare based on the livestock, fish, and produce around him. He joined in on fishing trips with local Vietnamese fishermen, excursions to the country to talk seed with farmers, and visited oyster luggers to understand varieties of oysters. He started a farm cooperative in Mississippi with local chefs Gerard Maras and Frank Brigtsen, raising quail, rabbits, and hogs. He wanted the hogs to make his own andouille sausage and ham. The Commander's Palace was now sourcing more and more food directly from the local land, from goat cheese to hot peppers. This was in the days when "farm-to-table" wasn't yet a food industry catchphrase, but the Commander's clientele were eating up the concept—and the food.

Working at Commander's Palace allowed Lagasse to explore New Orleans cuisine, but he also had the freedom to express himself. This resulted in the development of Emeril's signature style, which included innovative dishes like oysters in saffron cream sauce.

Emeril Delivers His Magic Touch

Meanwhile, the Brennans allowed Lagasse to experiment, giving him the opportunity to express himself — within bounds. Lagasse said that he was implementing his own style in a very discreet manner. In many ways, he knocked the kitchen down and built it back up again according to his own vision. He has said that he was set to take on the responsibility and develop his signature cuisine. On NOLA.com, Lagasse said, "The Brennans finally gave me a little window on the menu," he said. "I started doing local ingredients with a little more modern approach."[7]

For instance, over the objections of the Brennans, Lagasse put a rack of lamb with Creole mustard crust on the menu. It became a best seller. And soon customers started coming into the kitchen to quiz Lagasse on what specials they should order. Diners were introduced to quail, and they loved that as well. Emeril also concocted one of his all-time top recipes at Commander's Palace called smoked mushrooms and tasso over angel hair pasta.

Other successful dishes included the fish pompano, charcoal-broiled to a buttery turn and accompanied by a cream sauce infused with saffron and other herbs. There was also duck and wild mushroom gumbo, and plump crabmeat cakes, seasoned in a sauce of cream with oysters and their liquor. One night trout with pecans appeared on the menu, as well as a vegetable timbale (tim-baal), thick, custardy, and luscious. A starter of Oysters Trufant came delicately poached, crowned with a dollop of Oregon caviar and swathed in a cream sauce. Shrimp appetizers in butter, wine, and garlic, and shrimp in a seductive reduction of tomato, brandy, and shrimp essence were standouts. Turtle soup was always one of the favorites at Commander's and Emeril's version had a perfect balance of lemon and pepper that won rave reviews.

"New Orleans in the 1980s was a time of strong tradition," Lagasse said. "I never disrespected tradition. I always enhanced it."[8]

In an interview in NOLA.com, he said, "I began slowly falling in love with the city. Not only the food, but the people. Not only the people, but the music. The architecture, it made me feel like I was in Europe without being in Europe. One day, I decided this was the place."[9]

> *"I never disrespected tradition. I always enhanced it."*

While Lagasse was falling in love with New Orleans, his marriage was falling apart. When he moved his family south in 1982, he had two young girls Jessica (age 2) and Jillian (a newborn). But his relationship with his wife was now strained and she was not embracing New Orleans like Emeril was. Not long after arriving, Elizabeth told Emeril she was packing up the girls and moving back to Massachusetts. The Lagasses divorced in 1986 and Emeril dedicated his energies to work. In 1988, the restaurant guide Zagat's declared Commander's Palace to be the most popular restaurant in New Orleans.

A few year's after divorcing Elizabeth, Emeril met Tari Hohn, a fashion designer. They married in 1989. By the last two and a half years at Commander's Palace, he was not only the head chef but also the general manager. He ran the entire restaurant for the Brennan family. He was in charge of about 185 employees. He felt he had hit his peak at Commander's and there was nothing to do but to strike out on his own.

Making It Big
in the Big Easy

After about six years of working his culinary charms at Commander's Palace, Lagasse began to think about opening his own place. He had read the 1959 self-help classic *The Magic of Thinking Big* by David J. Schwartz and was influenced by its ideas. "It made me realize that people have big things in them," Emeril has said. "Sometimes they just need to be brought out. In order to be big, you have to think big. If you think small, you're going to be small."[1]

He also looked to his predecessor at Commander's Palace, superstar chef Paul Prudhomme. Prudhomme had left Commander's Palace, started his own successful restaurant, and his reputation had grown even bigger across the nation. Lagasse started to tell some people of his plan to open his own place. Many

"In order to be big, you have to think big. If you think small, you're going to be small."

thought he was crazy. He had one of the best-paying chef jobs in the country at one of the nation's top restaurants. Now he wanted to risk it all by opening his own place. He would basically have to go into debt to buy a place and go back to earning very little. Lagasse admitted it was a difficult decision to make but he knew it was time to move on.

Lagasse lived in the warehouse district of New Orleans. Across the street stood a burned-out building. Lagasse had a vision that he could convert the space into his own eatery. The neighborhood was changing. Galleries and other cultural venues were opening up. He saw that construction was beginning on some condominiums and apartment buildings in the area, but there was only one restaurant in the neighborhood. The warehouse zone was not the most traveled area, yet. There weren't any streetlights. There were no hotels. There wasn't even a grocery store in the neighborhood. Lagasse said, "You could shoot a cannon down Tchoupitoulas Street and not hit anybody."[2] Still, he felt the neighborhood had potential and that 800 Tchoupitoulas Street was calling to him. He thought the building would make a great restaurant.

Because he was such good friends with his employer, he told Ella Brennan of his plan. She supported him in leaving, but she thought it was crazy to open a restaurant in such a desolate location. She pushed for him to open in the French Quarter, an area visited by many tourists. Just as she was skeptical of his choice, so were many of the banks who turned down Lagasse's requests for a loan to get the business started. Needing to get financing, he suggested to Ella that they partner on the project. Ella, however, wasn't going to help if Lagasse insisted on the warehouse district. But his mind was made up.

Lagasse put everything he had into his first restaurant, Emeril's, located in an up-and-coming New Orleans neighborhood.

Launching his First Restaurant

Finally, Lagasse found a bank that would give him the financial backing. The bank was impressed with his plan—he had carefully developed the budgets, interior and kitchen design, customer base, and wine list. Although the bank was impressed, it wanted to be sure that Lagasse would be successful. A manager at the bank sought out a highly respected food critic to get his opinion on Lagasse. The critic told the bank that if there was anybody who was going to be successful, it would be Emeril Lagasse.

For eight months, he worked on the design and concept of his new place. Building began on the new restaurant in 1989. Lagasse felt the neighborhood could be dangerous at times, so he carried a gun. His new wife, Tari, helped come up with the interior design and even created an ice cream sandwich for the menu. Emeril put together the budget, the kitchen layout, and all other aspects of the restaurant. He chipped in on almost every level. He climbed the scaffolding and helped to paint the place. Although this was to be a white-tablecloth eating establishment for the locals, it also featured ten stools in a semicircle around a bar that gave a view into part of the kitchen. He wanted the kitchen to be part of the dining room and the dining room to be part of the kitchen. This is a style that has certainly spread since Lagasse opened his first place.

He also devoted a lot of time to the menu. Before he opened, he was spending about fifteen hours a day developing and testing the offerings, coming up with new classic dishes like barbecue shrimp, banana cream pie, and andouille-crusted redfish. Many were familiar dishes but Lagasse made them his own.

Even before he debuted Emeril's, the chef knew that he needed a dependable staff to succeed. A successful restaurant

★ The Funny Story of
Quail Milton

Lagasse needed to get the right permits to open his first restaurant and that could be a long, involved process. To help speed things along, it helped to win over local politicians. He made an appointment to see the councilman from his district, James Milton Singleton. Singleton could help Lagasse get the appropriate permits fast, so he could open on schedule. He had heard that Singleton loved quail. So on the date of their scheduled appointment, Lagasse walked in with a dish of stuffed quail with mushrooms, andouille, and a port wine sauce. Singleton devoured it and in a short time, Lagasse had the needed permits in his hand. To this day, he credits the dish for helping start his hit restaurant and if you ever do visit Emeril's, you should find Quail Milton on the menu.[3]

Lagasse and his wife Teri worked tirelessly to get Emeril's ready for opening day. But they hadn't counted on long lines of hungry diners waiting to get in. Despite a tumultuous opening, Emeril found his groove and the restaurant grew to be a huge success.

was the same as a successful sports team. Lagasse has said, "It's a team, and that's the way I look at it. I'm the quarterback, and we're all trying to win the Super Bowl."[4]

He handpicked a staff of thirty-three professionals from people he knew. He even stole away a general manager from Commander's Palace. Eric Lindquest helped him manage Emeril's restaurant then, and he helps direct Emeril's entire food empire today. As opening day approached, he and his staff would meet for what was basically show-and-tell. Staff could come and share information they thought was important about food and drink, as well as concerns and ideas.

March 24, 1990 was the big day. A recession had hit New Orleans hard, and the city hadn't seen a new restaurant open in about five years. Excitement was certainly building around Emeril's. Before the restaurant opened that night, Lagasse had one last training session with his staff. When he was sure that everyone and everything was set, he sent his team home to rest a little and get dressed. There were no advertisements or press releases announcing that Emeril's would open that day, but the news spread like wildfire through word of mouth. As the doors were being unlocked, a line of salivating customers had grown to epic proportions, snaking down the street. Some eager patrons had to wait ninety minutes before they could get in. The staff was so overwhelmed the first day that Lagasse closed the restaurant the next day just so they could all regroup and get their heads together. He decided that for the first few months at least Emeril's would only serve dinner because they had to get that right before moving on.

In the days to come, hungry diners would cram into his establishment to savor the caviar from the local choupique fish served on a fresh corn crêpe with crème fraiche. Many were

As Emeril's gained national recognition and critical acclaim, customers flocked to the restaurant to try Lagasse's unique take on classic New Orleans dishes. Lagasse became a culinary ambassador of New Orleans.

digging into the peppery étouffée of duck and wild mushrooms. (An étouffée is stew-like and served over rice.) Ravioli bulged with smoked chicken and sausage. A whole head of baked baby raddichio came stuffed with goat cheese. A crust of mustard, dill, tarragon, basil, cilantro and chive enlivened a pan-roasted salmon. A gumbo of rabbit and wild mushrooms was highlighted by a dark roux. The lobster arrived with Emeril's take on a Cajun maque-choux, which is a dish native to southern Louisiana consisting of a medley of corn, green bell pepper, onion, celery, and tomato. The banana cream pie with a banana crust and caramel left dessert fans swooning.

During the first two weeks, Lagasse basically kept his head down, working as more and more customers wanted to try the new exciting creations by this young chef. He had taken many of his dishes and food treatments from Commander's Palace and brought them to Emeril's. He was still committed to making everything from scratch, including the condiments. He was getting all his produce, meats, and fish locally. He was also overseeing every little detail in the early days. He checked the restrooms to make sure they had enough toilet paper and paper towels. And the neighborhood was still a little rough—he'd occasionally get calls that someone was trying to break into the place when it was closed.

Lagasse was so busy with the preparations that he forgot about a few essential things—such as how to pay his crew. Plus, he had been taking credit cards for payments and slips were piling up, but he hadn't been getting the funds into the bank. He hired Tony Cruz to handle the business end and it was soon operating smoothly.

In the early months of business, Lagasse got in the habit of waking up after just a couple of hours sleep. He would rise

When Lagasse needed a general manager to run his new restaurant, he selected Eric Lindquist (left), who had helped him manage Commander's Palace. Over time, Lagasse relied so heavily on the gifted Lindquist that he put him in charge of his food empire. Lindquist has been the president of Emeril's Homebase, which includes all of Lagasse's restaurants, food products, merchandise, and his foundation.

at five in the morning and head to the local vendors to buy his foods for the day. By 7 a.m., he was at the restaurant meeting with Lindquest to go over the menu and plans for the lunch and dinner ahead.

On a typical day at Emeril's, he gathers his staff together at about 5:30 p.m. The meeting begins with applause. The director of operations tells everyone how sales were at lunch. Then restaurant director goes over local events that might affect upcoming business, like special occasions or holidays. New staff members are introduced. Servers' fingernails and uniforms are inspected, and waiters present their corkscrews, pens and cigar cutters.[5] At six o'clock, the first seating comes in and it's time to go into full work mode until closing time. The kitchen often closes at 10:30, but after all is cleaned up, the restaurant might not lock its doors until 2:30 A.M. By the time Emeril gets home, it's only a few hours to sunrise and time to do it all again.

Hitting the Critical Jackpot

In New Orleans at the time, the critic to impress was Gene Bourg, who reviewed restaurants for The *Times-Picayune*. Instead of giving stars, Bourg awarded beans. Bourg's review of Emeril's appeared on August 30, a few months after the restaurant opened. A tough reviewer, Bourg had never awarded a restaurant his ultimate prize: five beans. When Lagasse got word that Bourg's review of Emeril's would be appearing in the paper, he was nervous but hopeful. Early in the morning before the sun had come up he sent a server out to fetch a copy. Lagasse and the staff hurried to the review page. They had hit the culinary jackpot: Emeril's had earned the coveted five beans. Bourg wrote: "Serious eaters had a right to expect the extraordinary when Emeril's materialized. Extraordinary is what they're getting, and it's being served up in spades."[6]

Now that he had his own place, Lagasse also wanted to follow his passion for wine that had started back when he was working at the Parker House. He had kept up his notebook of his thoughts on wines and now was his chance to share his tastes. When his new place opened, he had a wine list featuring about seventy-five different wines. In five years time, he had increased the choices to 500. In four more years, he offered a selection of 1,200.

Lagasse was always a stickler for details. In *The Reach of a Chef: Beyond the Kitchen*, Michael Ruhlman recalls a story from Emeril's culinary assistant Alain Joseph. One detail of Emeril's kitchen that he remembers is that there were no can openers in sight. They did use some canned food, but they didn't use the big table-mounted openers that many professional kitchens used. The chefs had to use their own handheld openers and use them out of customer view. Why? Because Emeril didn't want to give any impression that they were using any canned goods. Although they didn't use many, they had to use a few.[7]

By the end of the year, more praise was pouring in for Emeril's. John Mariani of *Esquire* magazine dubbed the eatery "Restaurant of the Year" in 1990. In 1991, *Wine Spectator* gave Emeril's its Grand Award. In 1991, the James Beard Foundation named Emeril as the Best Chef in the Southeast. That same year, *Food & Wine* magazine called Lagasse one of the top twenty-five new chefs in the country.

Lagasse's decision to open in the Warehouse District had proven right. The area underwent a huge upturn after Emeril's arrived and the location has continued to flourish with more residents, tourists, and commercial business. A contemporary

After the huge success of Emeril's, Lagasse opened a second restaurant, NOLA, in the famed French Quarter. NOLA offered both casual and elegant dining and the fare was to be "rustic Louisiana," which would allow Lagasse to expand his culinary repertoire.

arts center and children's museum have opened in the neighborhood. And Lagasse helped contribute to this revitalization with the start of his very first restaurant and then later establishing his corporate headquarters there.

Strike While the Iron Is Hot

Lagasse's success was snowballing and gaining momentum fast. He knew how to strike while the frying pan was hot, so to speak. So in 1992, just two years after opening Emeril's, the chef debuted NOLA (an acronym for New Orleans, Louisiana).

He and his wife, Tari leased a new space in the French Quarter. They promised the menu would not mimic Emeril's. The new eatery was meant to be a bit more casual and funky than his first enterprise. The second floor would offer some elegance with white tablecloths, but the ground floor was designed to be totally laid back with blond-wood chairs around bare tables. Tari again served as the interior designer, and she said that they wanted a space that would be comfortable for all types of people.

Rustic Louisiana cuisine was the star. The three-story restaurant offered diners an open-action kitchen, chef's food bar and a signature wood-fired brick oven. And the Lagasses set a price range at both lunch and dinner that would be more suitable for most middle-class wallets. Wines too were priced to be bargains and not break the bank. Dishes included andouille, sweet potatoes, boudin, beef brisket, pork chops and cornbread. Homemade pies shined and included coconut cream, lemon icebox, apple-buttermilk, and a chocolate-turtle pie with caramel sauce. With a big wood-burning oven on the premises, Lagasse could roast chickens or fire a jambalaya pizza. Chicken wings, crab cakes, pork cheek boudin balls, duck confit (con-

Between his work at Commander's Palace, Emeril's, and NOLA, Lagasse had gained a reputation as a talented, exciting chef. He was thrilled when this notoriety brought the legendary Julia Child to his restaurant. Child invited him to cook with her on her television show, and eventually Emeril reciprocated.

fee) and fried egg pizza, po boys, and cedar-plank roasted fish all attracted appreciative diners.

At NOLA, Lagasse also stuck to his guns about making items from scratch. Smoked meat, sausages, Worcestershire sauce, mozzarella and flavored ketchups were all made on the premises. NOLA was also great for the local economy. It was a big restaurant with a big staff. Emeril and Tari were employing seventy-five people there. In 1993, *Esquire* again lavished praise on Lagasse, choosing NOLA, his second restaurant, as the Best New Restaurant of the Year.

Emeril Lagasse was now on the national map. People from around the country were coming to see—and taste—what the fuss was all about. Even Billy Joel and Frank Sinatra stopped in at his first restaurant. Bruce Springsteen was a fan of his banana cream pie. Then one day, he learned that Julia Child planned to visit. Julia Child was one of the most popular, recognized chefs in the country. She often appeared on public television and demonstrated how to cook various dishes. When she was planning to visit Emeril's, Child had a show on PBS called *Cooking with the Master Chefs*. Lagasse dreamed of being on the program.

The day Child was to dine, his staff seemed exhausted and on low-boil, so to speak. He needed them to be energized, so he took them outside and told them that they were going to go for a jog. Many of his staff laughed when he suggested the idea, but they all went for a short run and the exercise gave them energy and revived their spirits. When Child came that night, she had a wonderful meal and she saw a lively joint and staff— just as Lagasse had hoped. Child was won over and taped a show featuring Lagasse and her preparing shrimp etouffee and boiled crawfish.

Television producer Geof Drummond said that even then, in 1992 when he taped his segment with Julia Child, Lagasse had that certain something extra that made him a star. In The *Cincinnati Enquirer* Drummond said that he may not have had the boldness that he developed later, but he had a generosity that came across on the small screen.[8]

Branching Out With Cookbooks

In 1993, Lagasse expanded his small but swiftly growing empire in a new direction. He published his first cookbook, *Emeril's New New Orleans Cooking*. It presented recipes for sautéed scallops with saffron corn sauce, stir-fry of sesame ginger crawfish over fried pasta, crabcakes with tomato mustard coulis, and chicken andouille hash and poached eggs. He shared his secrets for crawfish egg rolls with hot sesame drizzle, Big Easy seafood okra gumbo, pecan-encrusted lemon fish with lemon butter sauce, and piri piri chicken with jicama orange salad.

Of course, the dessert—banana cream pie with banana crust and caramel drizzle had to be included. This was Lagasse's chance to show the world his take on what he called Old New Orleans cuisine. The old style food was heavy, thick, and fried, and Lagasse thought he was bringing a lighter touch. He tried new flavor combinations. He brought an Indian touch to fish with curry-infused oil. He combined an Italian gnocchi (no-kee) with the local andouille sausage. His oysters Rockefeller were oysters with Pernod cream and fried spinach. He instructed readers to mix up their own home batches of Creole seasoning, Southwest seasoning, and stock ahead of time.

Also in 1993, Lagasse took to the road and traveled through the countryside of Louisiana so he could complete another book, *Louisiana Real and Rustic*. The book would hit the shelves in 1996 and be a bestseller.

Once Lagasse had built up his reputation, he turned to writing cookbooks. He published his first, *Emeril's New New Orleans Cooking*, in 1993. Today the prolific chef has authored 18 best-selling cookbooks—and there's no end in sight!

Chapter
5

Bam!
Emeril Becomes a Hit

I n 1994, the Food Network decided to try out another new show
with Lagasse as host. The new network had tried out Lagasse
the previous year, to near-disastrous results, on a show called
How to Boil Water. That show had been scripted and it did not
play to Lagasse's culinary strengths. They had also given him
a chance with another show called *Emeril and Friends.* Again,
Lagasse had seemed uncomfortable and exhibited none of the
personality he would later become known for. Fortunately, the
Food Network was so young and had almost nothing to lose, so
it was willing to try many new shows in order to find what its
audience responded to.

The new show was called *Essence of Emeril.* This show would
not be scripted, and Lagasse would be able to cook the Creole
foods he loved and felt comfortable with. He started filming in
New York and cracked that the whole studio smelled of shrimp
cocktail. The man from the Big Easy was finally at ease sharing
"kicked-up" recipes of his favorite foods.

The Food Network, which offered programming devoted solely to food, wanted Emeril. But the superstar chef had trouble being himself on camera.

With fewer boundaries, Lagasse seemed to develop a natural relationship with the viewers. Sometimes, his employees and friends would stop by to help prepare a dish. The show would start with some cool, mellow jazz. He made cilantro and coconut shrimp soup, boursin-stuffed chicken with a peppery Louisiana-style succotash, blue cheese pear strudel, caramelized onion cheesecake, vegetable tamale, roasted chili sauce, and a delightful eggplant caviar with a few basic ingredients. Sometimes he would share tips like how to cut ginger, cook pork tenderloin, or de-bone a squab. Lagasse said he was making about $50 a show and that the Food Network used to put him up in "dog hotels." He even had to bring his own coffee.

The show steadily caught on. In 1996, *Time* magazine dubbed *Essence of Emeril* one of the ten best shows on television. While it was a very good year for Lagasse professionally, his married life was falling apart. He and Tari Hohn divorced.

Marketing the Name

Lagasse also worked with the talent manager Shep Gordon, who helped grow his business. Gordon thought of a way to make Emeril more money. He thought Emeril could sell a product on his show that people would want to buy. The easiest and most sensible item, Gordon thought, would be spices. Gordon brokered a deal with the Food Network. They would film commercial spots selling Emeril's spice mixes. The spots would air during Lagasse's show and they would all share in the revenue. Eventually, sales skyrocketed and money from the spices came rolling in. [1]

Lagasse recognized that his name had selling power and it was a powerful brand in the cooking industry. He went on to form a partnership with All-Clad Metalcrafters to create

Lagasse took advantage of his superstar status to endorse his own line of food, cookware, and other products.

Emerilware gourmet pots and pans. The chef attached his name to salad greens and salad dressing. To serve the salad, a true Emeril fan could buy a special Emeril salad bowl. At one point, stores sold nine varieties of Emeril frozen shrimp and Emeril gourmet sausage. There were also Emeril pasta sauce, seasoning, and mustards. He had his own line of glassware, Emeril knives, and even Emeril-endorsed clogs. He went on to endorse floormats and toothpaste. All in all, about seventy grocery items feature Emeril's name.

Improvising Pays Off

Now that he was unscripted, he began to jazz up his delivery. When he added spice to a dish, he yelled "Bam!" which would become his signature. He also liberally used the phrases, "let's kick it up another notch," "yeah, baby!" "Hey, now!" and "pork fat rules!" Audiences knew his "holy trinity" of creole cooking: diced onion, celery and bell pepper. Lagasse would often throw a fourth into the trinity—one of his favorite ingredients—garlic. The French

> *"Let's kick it up to notches unknown by mankind."*

have a version of the holy trinity called mirepoix that replaces the bell pepper with carrot. On the rare occasions, Lagasse would suggest kicking things up to "notches unknown by mankind."

Lagasse said that people began shouting out his phrases at his restaurant. He knew they were catching on, but at some point one of the heads of the development thought he should lose the "Bam!" It's hard to imagine now, but that TV exec almost killed one of the 20th century's most popular catchphrases. In an interview on NPR, Allen Salkin, author of *From Scratch: Inside the Food Network,* said it would have been like taking "Ayyyyyy" away from the Fonz on the classic sitcom *Happy Days.*[2]

Back to the Restaurant Biz

With his new show doing so well, Lagasse was gaining nation-wide popularity. Las Vegas was booming as well. The city known for gambling was never a dining destination, but developers and investors thought that big-name chefs would enhance Las Vegas as a destination and please the high rollers who gambled there. Chef Wolfgang Puck may have led the charge when he opened Spago there in 1992. Soon, other top chefs opened restaurants in Las Vegas, including Bobby Flay, Alain Ducasse, Bradley Ogden, Nobu Matsuhisa, Thomas Keller, and Daniel Boulud.

Lagasse entered the Las Vegas arena in 1995 with Emeril's Fish House at the MGM Grand Hotel. Lagasse brought his Creole-inspired cuisine, such as barbecued shrimp, Louisiana-style étouffée, and oysters on the half shell with cucumber champagne mignonette. Sides like jalapeño cornbread, bacon mac 'n' cheese, and jambalaya made hearty accompaniments for Black Angus rib eye with warm remoulade sauce or crispy-skinned brick chicken.

In 1998, Lagasse again invested in the city that had done so much for him. A classic old New Orleans restaurant called Delmonico's had been shuttered in 1997. Delmonico's had been an institution in New Orleans for decades. It was renowned for its turtle soup and classic Creole dishes like chicken pontalba with its thick Bernaise sauce and ham and fried red fish. It was also famous for being a great steak house.

Emeril's products became incredibly popular, and he promoted them personally. Here, he promotes a special line of kitchen products and cookware sold exclusively at J.C. Penney Department Stores.

The restaurant had originated in New York in the 1827 and the owners opened this branch in New Orleans in 1895. The New York restaurant originated several recipes that became American classics, including eggs benedict, chicken a la king, Baked Alaska, and lobster Newburg. The New Orleans restaurant developed its own classics like Oyster Delmonico which offered raw oysters topped with crabmeat and melted cheese. Shrimp remoulade, trout amandine, and pompano en papillote highlighted the menu.

After about 100 years, the restaurant fell on hard times and on the day before Mardi Gras day in 1997, Delmonico's closed. The next day, a band gathered in front of the famous institution and played taps, the military music performed at funerals. Many, many people in New Orleans were sad to lose such a venerable institution. This was a fine dining establishment where people came to get engaged, celebrate birthdays, and recognize anniversaries. It looked like a piece of the city's history was dead.

Lagasse didn't want to see this great place go away, so he bought Delmonico's. In his cookbook *Emeril's Delmonico's,* the chef writes, "It was my vision to preserve the traditional and classic origins of the restaurant and pay homage to an establishment that had been in the community for 100 years. Here was a grande dame on stately St. Charles Avenue that just needed to be fluffed up, renovated, and redecorated to bring it into a new age, but I wanted to retain a certain uptown ambience and graciousness."[3]

Lagasse kept many of the classic items but added inventive flavors of his own. He had his housemade chorizo, oysters brochette, and Moris Kahn's Filet Mignon Tartar. Emeril's staff did tableside service and brought in fine wines. He made the restaurant elegant and understated, luxurious but comfortable.

Now firmly rooted in his adopted city of New Orleans, Lagasse invested in reopening Delmonico's, a classic restaurant and local favorite that had closed. He opened it as Emeril's Delmonico in 1998.

Listening:
⭐ A Key to Success

Success isn't always about being the loudest in the room and doing all the talking. Emeril and others who know him have said that his ability to listen to others has been a major factor in his success. Ella Brennan in The *Cincinatti Enquirer* said, "He's a sponge. Emeril soaks up information no matter where he is or what he does."[4]

Emeril believes that a good restaurateur has to be a good listener. He has attributed his success to listening and learning from those around him. By listening to others, he has drawn inspiration.

Kickin' It Up a Notch

Essence of Emeril was doing well in the ratings. One producer, though, thought of a new way to use the chef. The *Essence of Emeril* was not taped in front of a live audience, but occasionally guests asked if they could come in and view the show live. They had to hang in the shadows along a back wall. In taping so many shows, Emeril's energy would sometimes flag. But when guests came in, Emeril would perk up and be more lively. The producer thought that Emeril could have a very entertaining show in front of a live audience. People were recognizing that Emeril could be a real southern ham in front of a crowd, so the idea seemed natural. Lagasse, too, thought he would have more fun in front of a live audience. He thought he could be a David Letterman or Jay Leno—a type of entertaining talk show host but with a program centered around food. Lagasse also wanted to do a live show that would help promote his latest cookbook *Louisiana Real and Rustic*. So a plan was hatched to give a live Emeril program a try.

The Food Network in 1997 was still very low budget. They had a program called *Ready...Set...Cook!* that filmed in front of a live audience. On the show teams competed to prepare the best meal. The program was a sign of things to come as food competition shows would grow in popularity in the near future. To do the live show, producers thought that they would save money by taking advantage of the set for that show. They would give Lagasse a special program taped live in front of a studio audience focusing on recipes from his *Real and Rustic* cookbook. They would give it a try and see how it went. The idea was to make a cooking show as exciting and high energy as a rock and roll concert. They would start by taping this special and see where it would go from there.

Lagasse's fan base had been growing, but no one really had a full grasp of his popularity. On the taping of his first live special, Lagasse was shocked to arrive at the studio and see a huge crowd of adults and children. They were all excited and calling out to him. The TV set was decorated with touches from the bayou. The Cajun music put everyone in a party mood, and when Lagasse ran out at the beginning of the show, the crowd erupted with hoots and hollers. The Elvis of Cooking was in the building. Emeril wooed and yelled back to the audience. He was smiling ear to ear. He picked up a raw chicken on his cooking table and made it clap along with the crowd. Lagasse recalled that the crowd was almost hysterical and going crazy. None of the TV producers had ever heard a reaction like this. It just took that first taping for Food Network executives to realize that they may have a megawatt superstar on their hands.

The Food Network did the math and realized that a live show would be one of its most expensive shows to produce, but the channel decided to take a gamble. They offered Lagasse a new series where he would cook in front of a live audience. The series *Emeril Live* debuted on January 20, 1997 with Lagasse unscripted in front of a live audience. He had a two-piece band in the beginning, which eventually grew into a big band headed by Doc Gibbs. He opened with a monologue and then launched into the cooking. The show was a hit from the very start and ratings for his timeslot quickly doubled.

Emeril Live was incredibly popular and fans were very eager to get tickets. In the first year, the Food Network estimated that there were about half a million requests for tickets. The luckiest audience members got to snag a few of the seats that were directly attached to Lagasse's cooking station. These fortunate few were assured a taste of the master's delicacies. There were also about a half dozen café tables close to the cooking station—these folks would also often get a sampling from Lagasse's magic frying pan.

Lagasse would begin every show with an energetic charge out into the audience, pressing the flesh as if he were running for office. After a few remarks at the beginning, he would slip out of this sports jacket and into his chef's whites—jacket and apron—and the cooking would begin in earnest.

The short, solid fellow with big black caterpillar eyebrows and wavy black hair was very engaging when he was unscripted and charged up by the live audience. This program gave him a chance to do what he did best—talk to a crowd off the top of his head and from the heart. Maybe his musician instincts kicked in because Lagasse was incredibly good at improvising. The enthusiastic live audience seemed to boost the enthusiasm of the viewers at home. TV viewers could see people reacting to the smells, sounds and tastes of the food and it made the cooking that much more real.

Lagasse was easy-going and joking, so the program felt like being with a favorite uncle, and it made cooking seem friendly and unpretentious. His message was always to encourage anybody that they could do this. It wasn't rocket science. And his persona was appealing to all groups, young and old, women and men. He wasn't just the chef that housewives would watch in the afternoon. In fact, one episode he did was a "Manly Man" show where he prepared bacon wrapped pork chops and venison stew—and he passed out cans of beer to the audience to get them in the spirit of things.

He would say lines like, "We're just having too much fun and you should be with us here live in New York City!" and the audience would just erupt. Or he would enthusiastically add 35 cloves of chopped garlic to a pan and the audience would go absolutely nuts at this type of cooking bravado. Preparing food had never seemed so exciting.

In the *Boston Globe*, Doreen Iudica Vigue described the show as follows: "It's a mashed-potato Mardi Gras revel, complete with a live band and a host who acts as if he'd consider a warning from the cops proof of a good party. When the biscuits are ready, Lagasse doesn't just stack them on a serving plate; he tosses a few into the audience like a giddy peanut vendor at a ball game. It's Rocky Balboa with oven mitts, Fred Flintstone as the Galloping Gourmet. 'Hey!' he yells. 'This is like a real cookin' show we got here!'"[5]

An Unexpected Phenomenon

Lagasse had a crazy energy, one of his producers said that he could probably even sell hot dogs in the street. So he decided to try. He developed a character that was a cranky street guy. He filmed these man-in-the-street segments with unsuspecting strangers. He would push a food cart and sell his delicacies to unsuspecting customers, saying things like "What do you want? Come on, I ain't got all day. I got to go to work!" He pushed the act into different areas—taking it to Ringling Brothers and Barnum & Bailey Circus, for instance.

Emeril's catchphrases were also catching on like crazy. Full of energy, Emeril would take a pinch of spice or salt, wind up and pitch it into the pan with a yell of "BAM!" And the audience would shout "BAM!" along with him at the top of their lungs. The audiences ate up his over-the-top showmanship. "Let's dump in the whole bottle!" he'd say while cooking up some stew, or he'd speak to the frying pan as he added spice and say "Feel the love!" The audience would go into loud vocal fits of approval. This wasn't the subdued dump-and-stir programming of yesteryear. This was a whole new animal. People embraced his unique way of talking. They thrilled when he said "gahh-lick" in his distinctive Massachusetts accent. Even during commercial breaks, the chef was unflagging. Emeril would take over the drum kit and show off his chops. He knew how to play from his days on the high school drum team and he didn't mind showing off this extra dimension. Audiences were surprised that the master chef could also kill it on drums.

Lagasse and his producers recount one memorable show where he had a blast joking around and cooking a big baloney. He was swinging around this enormous cylinder of meat, and it wouldn't fit in the oven—the audience was howling with laughter. He once taught viewers how to make Urky Lurky, a pasta dish made from whatever leftovers were "lurking" in the refrigerator. In an interview with Martha Stewart, Emeril said, "I come from a basic philosophy: I work hard and I like to play hard." And that's exactly what he showed folks on his TV show.[6]

He brought on guests like Elmo from *Sesame Street*, Molly Shannon from *Saturday Night Live*, the musician Charlie Daniels, singer Patti Labelle, singer Michael McDonald, Joe Perry from Aerosmith, comedian Patton Oswald, and musician Jimmy Buffet. Other chefs would visit too—Alton Brown, Mario Batali, Julia Child, Bobby Flay and Jacques Pepin all stopped in to be "Bammed!" He had a Gospel Choir on one show that got the whole crowd swaying and clapping.

In 1997, Lagasse won the CableAce Award for Best Informational Series. In just a few months of doing *Emeril Live*, the chef was on fire with popularity. All the major newspapers and magazines were doing stories on him, including *Entertainment Weekly*, *Travel & Leisure*, *USA Weekend*, *Men's Journal*, *News-*

week, *Self, Esquire, Time, TV Guide, USA Today,* and *People.* He went on to appear on *The Tonight Show with Jay Leno,* NBC's *The Today Show, CBS This Morning,* and *Late Night with Conan O'Brien. Good Morning America* recognized a hot property when they saw one. The program asked him to come on as a food correspondent and he added that position to his already overwhelming schedule.

The Food Network recognized it had a hot property too and they wanted to get maximum mileage out of their star. Emeril was still taping *Essence of Emeril* for the daytime viewers and filming *Emeril Live* for the nighttime TV audience. Emeril was on television seven days a week. At its peak, *Emeril Live* aired every weeknight. Plus, the network had him making live appearances. Lagasse was the star of the network. In many ways, he *was* the Food Network. Lagasse enjoyed it all, but he also wanted time for his restaurants. The Food Network didn't want to lose Emeril.

Eventually, the Food Network cut Lagasse a record-breaking deal. The network that could barely afford to pay its talent in the beginning now offered the chef a million-dollar contract. It was unheard of. In a shrewd negotiating move, Lagasse requested all rights to *Emeril Live* and *Essence of Emeril* when he signed the contract. The Food Network didn't necessarily see a future value in the shows, so it agreed. But the programs would turn out to have great future worth.

With Fame Comes Backlash

Even at the height of his success, not everyone was thrilled with Lagasse in the food world. Many professional chefs believed his antics made a mockery of the profession.

Although he struggled in his early days with the Food Network, Lagasse found his stride with the unscripted live show *Emeril Live*. Cooking in front of a live audience brought out Emeril's energy, humor, and personality. Audiences loved the show, to which scoring a ticket was no easy feat.

In 1998, Amanda Hesser in *The New York Times* said that Lagasse worked his audience like a zookeeper, flinging them samples of salami and potato chips as he cooked. She was also critical of his overuse of "Bam!" noting that he seemed to be saying it every time he threw something in the pan or simply when he was at a loss for what to say. "He gives cooking an athletic quality, even if you wince every time you know a 'BAM!' is coming," wrote Hesser.[7]

She also criticized Lagasse for not giving many definite measurements. Emeril would say that you put the chicken in the water and cook it for "a very long time." Hesser also faulted his "kick-it-up" a notch approach, which often meant adding more garlic, bacon, or his own spice mix called *Essence of Emeril*. She pointed out that in his book *Emeril's TV Dinners*, his recipe for Southern-fried chicken required that chicken be seasoned at three different times with Essence of Emeril. In fact, many of the recipes in his cookbooks rely heavily on the use of Emeril's rubs or spice mixtures. Plus the man who was thought of as bringing a lighter touch to Southern cooking, seemed to veering back into a heavy touch— a very heavy touch. His love of pork fat wasn't exactly healthy. One of his mashed potato recipes could stop a heart if a person glanced at it—it called for a stick of butter, a cup of roasted garlic, and a cup of heavy cream.

Even John Mariani at *Esquire* magazine, who had named Lagasse one of the best chefs in the country, started to have a negative reaction to the show. He said that Lagasse's deliberate mangling of the English language grated on him.

Lagasse was stung by the criticism and defended his ways. He said that he wanted to show people that they could have fun in the kitchen, but still he took food seriously. Along the way, Lagasse thought he had taught audiences about many important food-related topics, such as cooking according to the seasons, farmers, organic foods, locally grown produce, and local traditions. "I was really hurt when [Hesser's] article first came out," he said in the The *Cincinnati Enquirer.* "But all my colleagues called ... and they told me it was just her opinion. I got over it."[8] He stuck to his belief that people want to be entertained. Plus, he added that people could get the details for the recipes by visiting the website later.

6

The Empire
Strikes Back

The negative criticism of Lagasse had no effect on his popularity. In 1999, he published another cookbook, *Every Day's a Party*. (In 1997, he had put out *Emeril's Creole Christmas* and *Emeril's TV Dinners* in 1998.) As he toured the country to promote his latest book, attendance records were broken at many bookstores. It was not unusual for 2,000 to 3,000 people to come and wait hours to see him. They'd come wearing Emeril hats and T-shirts. Many would bring gifts such as home-baked cookies or stuffed animals.

For most chefs, the traditional audience had been women. Lagasse did attract a female following, but men were also interested in his show and so were children. He had an amazing way of appealing to all groups of people. In total, he has written eighteen cookbooks. One of his latest books, published in 2013, was titled *Cooking with Power*.

He was chosen as "Chef of the Year" by *GQ* magazine in 1998 and the following year he was named one of *People* magazine's "25 Most Intriguing People of the Year." In 1999, he opened

Emeril's Orlando at Universal Studios City Walk and Delmonico Steakhouse in the Venetian Resort, Hotel & Casino in Las Vegas. By 2000, Emeril's restaurant empire had grown as well. He had six restaurants and 975 employees.

Because his first Orlando restaurant was a hit, Lagasse returned to the city and started another eatery at Universal Orlando. Called Tchoup Chop (pronounced chop-chop), the new venue referred to New Orleans' famous Tchoupitoulas Street but the menu featured a fusion of Asian and Polynesian foods, such as steamed dumplings, ahi poke rice bowl, and udon noodles. He also kicked off Emeril's Atlanta in 2003. Unfortunately, the business couldn't generate enough profit over time and it closed in 2008. By 2005, however, Lagasse would have 1,500 employees working at his restaurants alone. Many of the employees had stayed with him for years. He was known as a kind and generous boss who rewarded hard work. Today, he has more than 1,800 people working for him.

In *USA Today*, Lagasse said, ""I know that I'm responsible for a lot of people eating, and sleeping. But then you add an average person that has two to three people in their family. So I equate that to around maybe 5,000 people that I'm responsible for."[2]

A natural restaurateur, Lagasse continued to build up new eateries. In February 2008, he opened Table 10 at The Palazzo in Las Vegas. Then he started his first restaurant in the Northeast, Emeril's Chop House in 2009 at the Sands Casino Resort Bethlehem in Pennsylvania. That same year, he was back in Las Vegas to kick off Lagasse's Stadium, a restaurant and sports entertainment venue at The Palazzo. Also in 2009, he tried his hand at hamburgers, opening his first-ever burger restaurant called Burgers And More by Emeril back at the Sands Casino,

Treating
★ Employees Right

Emeril attributes a lot of his success to the people he hires. Some of his employees have been with him for decades. He also believes in giving workers a chance to succeed. Bernard Carmouche started out as a dishwasher at Commander's Palace at age 17. Orignally, all he wanted was to earn $200 to buy a Dodge Dart. One day, however, he asked the chef if he could teach him to cook. Emeril said he would if he finished high school first. When Carmouche finished school and showed Emeril his report card, the chef put him on duty making salads. As he proved himself, Carmouche moved up the ranks. He worked the hot line, the back line, as first chef and as sous chef at Commander's. He finally worked his way up at age thirty to chef de cuisine at Emeril's. By age 44, he was culinary director for three of Lagasse's Florida restaurants. At age 47, he opened his own restaurant in Orlando. "Whatever is taught to you, you teach the next person," said Carmouche in the *Orlando Sentinel*. "Mentoring is a gift not to keep, but to pass on."[1]

No matter how successful is, Lagasse refuses to rest on his laurels. Along with his television shows and merchandising, he continues to open new and diverse restaurants, including Table 10 in Las Vegas.

In 2000, Emeril married southern belle Alden Lovelace. The couple has two children, daughter Meril and son E.J. The Lagasse family mixes business with pleasure and charity.

Bethlehem. In 2011, he introduced his first-ever Italian restaurant, Emeril's Italian Table—again at the Sands casino in Bethlehem. In January 2012, he opened his newest restaurant, e2 emeril's eatery in Charlotte, North Carolina.

Love and Charity Come Calling

With this busy a life, it almost seemed impossible to have a love life. But along the way, Emeril met Alden Lovelace. Lovelace was a true southerner who grew up in Gulfport, Mississippi. She graduated from the University of Mississippi with a bachelor's degree in journalism in 1989. On their first date, he took her to eat mussels at La Crepe Nanou in uptown New Orleans. The two fell in love and were married in 2000. They had two children shortly thereafter: a son, Emeril John (E.J.) Lagasse IV, born in March 2003 and a daughter Meril Lovelace Lagasse, born in December of 2004. (Note that Meril's name is just one letter shy of her father's name.)

"You also have to be able to laugh with one another even if sometimes that means laughing at yourself. I'm very blessed because I truly feel I married my best friend."

Lagasse hoped this third time would be a charm. Alden shared the secret to their long-lasting relationship on the website *Sip & Savor*: "I think at the end of the day you need to have friendship and respect at the core. Good chemistry doesn't hurt either! You also have to be able to laugh with one another even if sometimes that means laughing at yourself. I'm very blessed because I truly feel I married my best friend and we have a lot of fun together."[3]

Alden has also guided Emeril into more philanthropic endeavors. In 2002, the couple cofounded the Emeril Lagasse Foundation. Much of her time with the foundation is dedicated to creating and developing ideas that generate new educational opportunities for children, especially those who are disadvantaged. She's also helped raise money for a local children's museum in New Orleans. Through the foundation, the couple also mentors young people in the culinary arts. The organization has distributed more than six million dollars in grants to children's charities. A few of the projects funded by the Emeril Foundation include an accessible learning kitchen for special needs students at St. Michael Special School, and an outdoor classroom, gardens, fresh foods cafeteria and teaching kitchen at Edible Schoolyard New Orleans. Emeril and Alden raise money for the foundation through Carnivale du Vin, a huge charity wine auction.

The Foundation also generates funding by holding the annual Boudin, Bourbon and Beer Festival of Music and Food. In March 2011, Lagasse dedicated the Emeril Lagasse Foundation Culinary Arts Studio, a four-year culinary arts program for high school students with master-apprentice curriculum at New Orleans Center for the Creative Arts. For his charitable efforts, the James Beard Foundation named Emeril Humanitarian of the Year in 2013.

Although much of their work is based in New Orleans and New York, Emeril and Alden eventually moved their family to Destin, Florida. Alden's family had strong ties to that area. Plus, Emeril has been a big fisherman and he loves to fish the Northwest Florida Gulf Coast as often as he can. On Sundays when

Lagasse's success has taken him in some unexpected directions, including the world of acting. In 2001, he starred in a short-lived eponymous sitcom on the NBC network.

he's home and relaxing, what does Emeril do? He cooks a big dinner for family and friends.

Trying to Cook Up a Comedy

In 2001, Lagasse was getting bigger and bigger as a celebrity. When TV producers approached him about doing a sitcom on NBC, he thought why not give it a try. He filmed thirteen episodes of the half-hour sitcom called *Emeril*, but doing comedy was not in the cards for the chef.[4] For many critics, the show was missing an essential ingredient—humor. *People* magazine said that Lagasse was very engaging but having a good personality didn't necessarily make someone a good actor. Some pointed out that Lagasse was short and every other cast member was taller than he was. Also, the show debuted just two weeks after 9/11. Lagasse has said that even *Seinfeld* wouldn't have been able to have a hit comedy during that time when the nation was reeling from the aftermath of terrorist attacks. TV audiences, however, did turn more to the Food Network during that period, seeking the comforts of home and home cooking. By November of 2001, Emeril's comedy was off the air.

Lagasse's manager said that although the sitcom failed, the chef had gained a wider audience, and his popularity on the Food Network continued to soar. In 2003, the Food Network renewed his contract and called him "the cornerstone" of the channel. He went on to do memorable specials in Orlando, Las Vegas, and even one at the Eastern State Penitentiary in Pennsylvania.

Bringing Back Business After the Hurricane

New Orleans suffered a huge blow in 2005 when Hurricane Katrina hit. The tourism industry took a huge downturn. The

Lagasse has used his success to embark on several charity ventures. His Emeril Lagasse Foundation provides opportunities for disadvantaged youth. Legasse also mentors and inspires young people who want to work in the hospitality and food services industries.

people of New Orleans were hurting. But Lagasse, like so many other chefs in the area, remained dedicated to the city and helping it come back to life. Today, there are more than twice the number of places to eat than before the hurricane hit. Lagasse's restaurants still attract a huge number of visitors and that meant jobs and tax revenue for the city.

His corporate office is called Emeril's Homebase, and that too is located in New Orleans. It is located in a converted bowling alley that is now a state-of-the-art facility, with a test kitchen and library. Administrative staff, test kitchen workers, writers, marketers, web managers and other professionals all work from these headquarters. From his headquarters, Lagasse could review all the details of his swiftly expanding empire.

Chefs need to be able to prepare several dishes at once and keep their eye on different burners as food cooks, and Lagasse always had an uncanny knack to keep an eye on all parts of his business. His business manager, Tony Cruz, once said that Emeril could look at a report on expenses and instantly recognize if costs were too high. In *Cigar Aficionado*, Cruz said, "He's absolutely on top of profit and loss. He is a very smart businessman."[5]

In the same year as Katrina, Lagasse continued to grow his business. He signed a deal with the Shop at Home cable network, and began hosting a weekly show called *From Emeril's Kitchen*. Scripps owned both The Food Network and the Shop at Home network, so Emeril could be on both channels without a conflict. In addition to this weekly show, he would do a few specials for the channel as well, and through all the programming, he would be selling kitchen wares.

Chapter 7

End of an Era
and New Beginnings

By 2007, *Emeril Live* had completed a ten-year run. The initial excitement of the show was starting to wear thin. Emeril was losing some of his sizzle. In the beginning, a show with a dynamite host who showed home viewers how to cook was all that the network needed. Lagasse was a good time and people in the live audience and home audience fed off that energy. The Food Network loved him too and usually consulted him about programming.

Allen Salkin details the decline of Lagasse's popularity in his book *From Scratch: Inside the Food Network*. The network was moving forward when Brooke Johnson became president in 2004. One of her first moves was to organize a study of the network to find out what was working and what was not.

The results of the study showed that people were viewing the network as unexciting. Most of the programming was labeled as "dump-and-stir" shows. The format of many of the shows was the same—the chef talks and demonstrates how to make a dish. The report showed that other networks were stealing audiences away with more dynamic programming. Reality shows and travel programs were drawing more viewers.

The message from the study on the Food Network was to start changing or fade away. Lagasse had such a long and stable history with the channel that he wasn't going out the door immediately. Gradually, the network was introducing newer programming designed to appeal to a younger audience. Shows like *Iron Chef* imported from Japan, brought a campy cooking competition to the air and it proved to be a smash, especially with younger viewers. The program pitted a respected chef against one of the Iron Chefs on the show. Alton Brown's *Good Eats* explored the science, history, and techniques behind foods—all with a good dose of humor. Bobby Flay's competition show *Throwdown* was drawing younger and bigger audiences than *Emeril Live*. Research showed that other networks were luring in bigger audiences with more exciting programming—like the competition show *Top Chef* on Bravo. Shows that were filmed in a studio were declining in appeal.

For Johnson, the message was clear: Lagasse's star was fading. Also, his show was more expensive to produce than many of the younger hipper shows that were coming down the pipeline. Salkin reported that a whole 13-show series of a new program cost one week of Emeril's show. Also, *The New York Times* reported in 2007 that Food Network's ratings were dipping during some blocks of programming and that was costing the channel. Advertisers bought time priced according to how many viewers were being reached. If viewership was lower than promised, the Food Network had to give refunds to the advertisers, known as "make goods." These amounted to financial losses for the network. "All good things come to an

Lagasse's good friend Bobby Flay go way back to the early days of the Food Network. While Emeril stuck to what he did best, Flay created new shows that changed with the network's audience. The result was that Emeril's ratings dropped, while Flay became a Food Network superstar.

end, and it was time to do something new," said Brooke Johnson in The *New York Times*.[1]

So in 2007, Johnson broke the difficult news: the network was considering canceling *Emeril Live*. Lagasse took the news in disbelief. He couldn't believe it because he was the anchor—he was on the channel all the time. He was a crucial part of the Food Network identity. Bobby Flay understood that he had to change and adapt in this food media world. He pitched many show ideas. But Emeril wasn't one for drumming up new ideas, and he didn't really think cancellation would happen. Those on his side thought he might give his reputation and image a lift by competing on *Iron Chef America*. But Lagasse really wasn't the type to be portrayed as a fierce competitor. He thought going on such a show was a demotion—he didn't see it as a way to recast himself and make himself popular with a younger audience.

Without his show, Lagasse was saddened and confused but he threw himself back into what he knew best—cooking. He returned to his restaurant in New Orleans. He mulled over what was happening. He was uncertain what direction to take next.

Although he had left the Food Network disheartened, he had the last laugh so to speak. Ages ago, he had negotiated contracts that had given him the rights to all the old shows that he had filmed with the Food Network. He sold everything to do with Emeril, except his restaurants, to Martha Stewart Living Omnimedia for $50 million.

You Can't Keep a Good Man Down

As can be expected, Lagasse wasn't about to stay away from TV. In 2008, he did a series for the Discovery Channel set in Whole Foods Market. In 2009, he began guest judging on Bravo TV's hit *Top Chef*. *Top Chef* was a highly rated program and the

Food Network had tried many times to come up with a something similar but they could never get the formula right. Seeing Lagasse on *Top Chef* may have made a few executives at Food Network regret letting him go. In 2010, he went on to host a variety show on Ion Television.

In a strange twist, however, Lagasse would return to the Food Network family. Scripps, which owned the Food Network, decided that it needed another television network that would be grittier, edgier, and hipper than the Food Network. They also wanted a network that would be more serious about food and cooking, which the Food Network had moved away from. So in 2010, the Cooking Channel was launched. The Cooking Channel decided to turn back to Emeril. He began hosting *Fresh Food Fast*, a program where he prepared healthy, easy meals. "The cool thing is that now that people have made this evolution where cooking is cool, people are doing it on weekends, they're doing their own challenges," Lagasse told *USA Today* while marketing and filming in New York City. "It's back to cooking. And it's real cooking."[2]

He also filmed *The Originals* for the Cooking Channel, a show about food establishments that have helped shape America's culinary landscape. In 2013, he was taping another show for Cooking Channel called *Emeril's Florida*.

Also in 2013, he launched a daytime program called *Emeril's Table* on the Hallmark Channel. On the show, Lagasse cooked while five guests sat in his kitchen asking culinary questions, trading tips and recipes, and of course, eating. If TV viewers couldn't get enough Emeril in human form, they could also tune into the animated series *Futurama*. The alien Chef Elzar on the show is a parody of Emeril.

Emeril is a valued judge and mentor on the Bravo network's award-winning cooking competition *Top Chef.* Pictured here with *Top Chef* host Tom Colicchio, Emeril's presence was particularly felt during Season 11, when the show taped in New Orleans.

Over time, Lagasse has become such an iconic American chef that the Smithsonian even displays one of his chef's jackets at the National Museum of American History. As far as the future is concerned, Emeril shows no signs of slowing down. He has an insatiable curiosity, a love of people, and a passion for cooking that keeps him going. In *Details* magazine in the spring of 2015, he said, "My philosophy is still the same as it has been since day one in that I want to get up and I want to be a little bit better than I was the day before. And so however I need to do that, *that* is what I try to focus on. I don't believe in wasting time. I don't believe in wasting knowledge. I tell my people that if they are not learning something every day, they are cheating themselves. Because in this business, there is so much out there to learn. At least that's how I go about it."[3]

> *"My philosophy is still the same as it has been since day one in that I want to get up and I want to be a little bit better than I was the day before."*

Becoming a Chef

For many, the path to becoming a chef is similar to Emeril Lagasse's career. You have to learn the skills by doing. Work experience is the main ingredient. Many top chefs like Lagasse, Bobby Flay, Anthony Bourdain, Michael Mina, Grant Achatz, David Chang, and Todd English all went to culinary school. Mario Batali attended London's Cordon Bleu for a short time but dropped out, deciding he would learn more from great

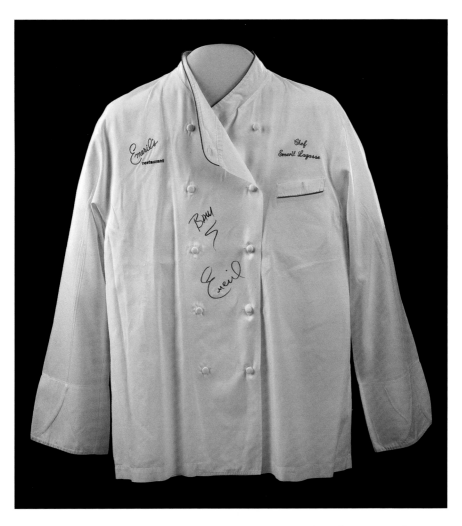

Emeril has become such a symbol of cooking in the United States that his chef's coat is on display at the Smithsonian National Museum of American History in Washington, DC, complete with his autograph and signature word: Bam!

The Importance of
a Mentor

Emeril believes that for a young chef to succeed a mentor is essential. In an interview in *Details* magazine, Emeril said, "I think you should have a mentor—at least one mentor. It doesn't necessarily have to be a chef, but there should be someone out there that you are really inspired by, not only from a business perspective but certainly from a culinary perspective, too. And I think you need to read as much as you can."[4]

Emeril Lagasse knew from an early age that he wanted to make food his life's passion. Lagasse pursued a formal education in the culinary arts, but that is not the only way to become a chef.

chefs who were working at top restaurants. Pro chefs Ashley Christensen, Barbara Lynch, and Susan Goin did not go to culinary school. By just learning on the job, they paved their way to success.

While culinary school isn't necessary, it can provide an aspiring chef with the skills needed to enter a kitchen and perform from the get-go. Even knowing the language of cooking (names of sauces, methods of heating, etc.) can go a long way when entering a professional kitchen. Most programs cover all the basics when it comes to working in a restaurant. Beyond cooking techniques (like knife skills) and kitchen operations, culinary school courses cover menu planning, food sanitation procedures, and purchasing and inventory methods. Most training programs also require students to get real-world experience. Through connections from their schools, students may complete internships or apprenticeships in commercial kitchens.

Some community colleges and technical schools also offer professional training in cooking. More than 200 academic training programs at post-secondary schools are accredited through the American Culinary Federation (ACF). The ACF also organizes certification programs—chefs that receive certification demonstrate that they have reached a certain level of competence. Students should keep in mind that cooking school can be expensive and may require paying back loans for years to come.

The Bureau of Labor Statistics lists the following talents as being important to succeeding:

Business skills. Many chefs run their own business or are in charge of the finances at a restaurant. They can benefit from learning how to handle administrative tasks, such as accounting and personnel management, and be able to manage a restaurant efficiently and profitably.

Communication skills. Chefs need to be able to communicate quickly and clearly with their staff to make sure food is being executed properly and brought to the tables in an efficient manner.

Creativity. The chefs who truly shine come up with their own dishes. They take time to be creative and develop interesting and innovative recipes. They should be able to use various ingredients to create appealing meals for their customers.

Dexterity. For chefs and head cooks, their job depends on fast, clean and precise cutting techniques. It's all in the hands—so manual dexterity is a must.

Leadership skills. Chefs need to motivate, instruct, and organize kitchen staff to get meals completed and served. Developing a cooperative atmosphere of staff is an essential skill.

Try It Yourself!

Blackened Redfish

Serves 4

Ingredients

1 tablespoon (15 mL) smoked paprika

2 ½ teaspoons (12 mL) salt

1 teaspoon (5 mL) onion powder

1 teaspoon (5 mL) garlic powder

1 teaspoon (5 mL) cayenne

¾ teaspoon (4 mL) black pepper

¾ teaspoon (4 mL) chili powder

½ teaspoon (2.5 mL) dried thyme

½ teaspoon dried oregano

12 ounces (350 g), (2 sticks) butter, melted

(6) 8 ounce (230 g) skinless, boneless red
    snapper, red drum, or perch filets, ½"-thick

Lemon juice, to taste

Directions

1.) Mix together herbs and spices, stirring until well blended.

2.) Put butter into a wide, shallow bowl. Dip each filet in butter and place on a sheet pan.

3.) Dust each filet generously on both sides with spice mixture, pressing the seasonings into fish with your fingers. Save remaining butter.

4.) Heat a large cast-iron skillet over high heat until very hot— 8-10 minutes. Make sure your cooking space is well ventilated.

5.) Carefully place 2-3 filets in pan. They should sizzle. Stand back to avoid splatter and smoke.

6.) Pour 1 tsp. of the remaining butter over each filet. Cook until bottom of each filet appears charred, about 2 minutes. Turn filets over and pour 1 tsp. butter over each. Continue cooking until fish is cooked through (about 3-4 minutes).

7.) Serve with melted butter and lemon juice.

Sausage and Kale Soup

Serves 6

Ingredients

1 tablespoon (15 mL) olive oil

1 tablespoon (15 mL) minced garlic

½ cup (120 mL) diced onions

½ cup diced turnips or parsnips

½ cup diced carrots

1 bunch kale, de-stemmed and roughly chopped

¾ cup (170 g) sliced andouille, chorizo, or hot Italian sausage

3 bay leaves

2 tablespoons (30 mL) chopped fresh parsley leaves

2 tablespoons fresh thyme, pulled from stem

6 cups (3 pints) beef, chicken, or vegetable stock

1 cup (240 mL) red kidney or white beans

6 ounces (170 g) diced tomatoes

3 large potatoes, diced

Directions

1.) Heat oil in a large stock pot over medium-high heat. Add garlic, onions, turnips and carrots and cook for 5 minutes, or until onions begin to turn translucent.

2.) Add the kale, chorizo, bay leaves, parsley and thyme and stir well. Add stock, beans and tomatoes.

3.) Bring the soup to a boil, and reduce the heat to low. Simmer for at least 30 to 40 minutes.

4.) In a medium saucepan, bring salted water to a boil and add the diced potatoes. Cook until tender, about 10 minutes. Drain the potatoes and add them to the soup.

5.) Remove the bay leaves and serve hot with some crusty, buttered bread.

Jalapeño Cheddar Cornbread

Serves 8

Ingredients

16 ounces (2 boxes) (320g) cornbread mix

2 eggs, lightly beaten

²/₃ cup (160 mL) low-fat milk

8 ounces (240 mL) sharp cheddar, shredded (about 2 cups)

1 cup (150 g) canned corn, drained

2 jalapeño peppers, seeded and minced

Directions

1.) Heat oven to 400°F (205°C).

2.) Lightly coat a 13-by-9-inch baking pan with vegetable cooking spray.

3.) Combine the corn-bread mix with the eggs and milk. Stir in the cheddar, corn, and jalapeños.

4.) Pour into pan and bake 12 to 15 minutes or until the top is golden.

Banana Cream Pie

Serves 6

Ingredients

$1/3$ cup (80 mL) flour

$2/3$ cup (160 mL) sugar

2 egg yolks

2 cups (475 mL) half-and-half (or whole milk)

1 teaspoon butter

$1^1/2$ teaspoons vanilla

2 bananas, sliced

1 baked pie crust

$1/2$ cup (120 mL) whipping cream

$1/4$ cup (50 g) sugar

111

Directions

1.) In medium heavy saucepan, mix flour, sugar, yolks and half and half.

2.) Cook and stir until mixture comes to a boil. Let boil for 1 minute.

3.) Add butter and vanilla.

4.) Place half the bananas in bottom of baked pie crust.

5.) Pour half the filling over bananas.

6.) Repeat layers until custard and bananas are all used.

7.) Cover with wax (or parchment) paper and chill.

8.) Whip the cream with mixer on high until stiff peaks form. Stir in the sugar.

9.) Pile whipped cream on top of your pie.

10.) Slice and enjoy!

New Orleans-Style Barbecued Shrimp

Serves 6

Ingredients
_____

4 pounds unpeeled, jumbo fresh shrimp or
    6 pounds shrimp with heads on

¹⁄₂ cup (120 g) butter

¹⁄₂ cup (120 mL) olive oil

¹⁄₄ cup (60 mL) chili sauce

¹⁄₄ cup Worcestershire sauce

2 lemons, sliced

4 garlic cloves, chopped

2 tablespoons (30 mL) Creole seasoning (such
    as Paul Prudhomme's or Tony Chachere's)

2 tablespoons lemon juice

1 tablespoon chopped parsley
1 teaspoon (5 mL) paprika
1 teaspoon oregano
1 teaspoon ground red pepper
$\frac{1}{2}$ teaspoon hot sauce
Baguette (French bread)

Directions

1.) Spread shrimp in a shallow, aluminum foil-lined broiler pan.

2.) Combine butter, lemon juice, Worcestershire sauce, chili sauce, and spices in a saucepan over low heat, stirring until butter melts.

3.) Pour mixture over shrimp.

4.) Cover and chill for 2 hours, turning shrimp every 30 minutes.

5.) Bake, uncovered, at 400°F (205°C) for 20 minutes; turning once.

6.) Peel shrimp and serve with bread.

Roasted Garlic Cauliflower

Serves 4

Ingredients

2 tablespoons (30 mL) minced garlic

3 tablespoons (45 mL) olive oil

1 large head cauliflower, separated into florets

Salt, pepper, to taste

½ cup (120mL) grated parmesan cheese

¼ cup (60mL) chopped fresh parsley

Directions

1.) Preheat the oven to 450°F (233°C).

2.) Grease a large casserole dish.

3.) Place the olive oil and garlic in a large resealable bag. Add cauliflower, and shake to mix.

4.) Pour into the prepared casserole dish, and season with salt and pepper to taste.

5.) Bake for 25 minutes, stirring halfway through.

6.) Top with Parmesan cheese and parsley, and broil for 3 to 5 minutes, until golden brown.

SELECTED RESOURCES BY EMERIL LAGASSE

Books

Emeril 20-40-60 Fresh Food Fast. New York: William Morrow and Company, 2009.

Emeril's Delmonico. New York: HarperCollins, 2005.

Emeril's There's a Chef in My World: Recipes That Take You Places. New York: HarperCollins, 2006.

Farm to Fork: Cooking Local, Cooking Fresh. New York: HarperCollins, 2010.

Louisiana Real and Rustic. New York: William Morrow and Company, 1996.

Sizzling Skillets and Other One-Pot Wonders. New York: HarperCollins, 2011.

Websites

www.Emerils.com

Restaurants

Delmonico Steak House

Emeril's Delmonico

Emeril's New Orleans

Emeril's New Orleans Fish House

Emeril's Orlando

Emeril's Tchoup Chop

Lagasse's Stadium

NOLA Restaurant

Table 10

CHRONOLOGY

⭐

October 15, 1959 — Born in Fall River, Massachusetts.

1969 — Works at Portuguese bakery.

1977-78 — Attends Johnson & Wales College of Culinary Arts.

1978 — Marries Elizabeth Kief.

1979 — Hired as executive chef at Dunfey's Hyannis Resort in Cape Cod, Massachusetts.

1980 — Jessica Lagasse is born.

1982 — Hired as executive chef at Commander's Palace in New Orleans.

1982 — Jillian Lagasse is born.

1986 — Divorces Elizabeth Kief.

1989 — Marries Tari Hohn.

1990 — Opens Emeril's Restaurant in New Orleans.

1990 — *Esquire* names Emeril's "Restaurant of the Year."

1991 — Named the James Beard Foundation Best Chef in the Southeast.

1992 — Opens NOLA.

1993 — Publishes first cookbook, *Emeril's New New Orleans Cooking.*

1993 — Stars in first Food Network Series, *How to Boil Water.*

1993 — *Emeril and Friends* airs.

1994 — *Essence of Emeril* debuts.

1996 — Divorces Tari Hohn.

1997 — *Emeril Live* debuts.

1998 — Opens Emeril's Delmonico's.

1998 — Named "Chef of the Year" by *GQ* magazine.

1999 — Named one of *People* magazine's "25 Most Intriguing People of the Year."

1999 — Opens Emeril's Orlando at Universal Studios City Walk and Delmonico Steakhouse in the Venetian Resort, Hotel & Casino in Las Vegas.

2000 — Marries Alden Lovelace.

2002 — Founds the Emeril Foundation.

2003 — Son Emeril John Lagasse IV is born.

2004 — Meril Lovelace Lagasse is born.

2007 — *Emeril Live!* is canceled.

2008 — Martha Stewart Living Ominimedia buys the Emeril brand.

2009 — Appears for first time as guest judge on *Top Chef.*

2010 — Begins appearing on Cooking Channel.

2013 — *Emeril's Florida* debuts.

2013 — James Beard Foundation names Lagasse Humanitarian of the Year.

CHAPTER NOTES

Chapter 1: A Chef at an Early Age

1. Brainquote.com. http://www.brainyquote.com/quotes/quotes/e/ emerillaga214373.html (accessed June 1, 2015).
2. Grossman, John. "Recipe for Success." *Cigar Aficionado.* January/ February 1998. http://www.cigaraficionado.com/webfeatures/ show/id/Recipe-for-Success_6067 (accessed June 1, 2015).
3. Lagasse, Emeril. *Emeril's New New Orleans Cooking.* (New York: William Morrow Cookbooks, 1993.)

Chapter 2: Full Speed Ahead

1. Shrieves, Linda. "Essence of Emeril." *Orlando Sentinel.* May 6, 1999. http://articles.orlandosentinel.com/1999-05-06/lifestyle/ 9905050496_1_emeril-lagasse-essence-of-emeril-orlan- do-restaurant
2. Qotd.org. http://www.qotd.org/search/single.html?qid=33904 (accessed May 25, 2015).
3. "Emeril Lagasse: Five Things I Can't Live Without." *Restaurant Hospitality.* April 20, 2015. http://restaurant-hospitality.com/ chef-interviews/emeril-lagasse-5-things-i-cant-live-without (accessed May 25, 2015).
4. Witkowski, Robert. "Acadia's Cajuns." *Portland Monthly.* Summer Guide 2010. http://www.portlandmonthly.com/portmag/2010/06/ acadias-cajuns (accessed May 25, 2015).

Chapter 3: A Song of the South

1. Grossman, John. "Recipe for Success." *Cigar Aficionado.* January/ February 1998. http://www.cigaraficionado.com/webfeatures/ show/id/Recipe-for-Success_6067 (accessed June 1, 2015).
2. Turner, Marcia Layton. *Emeril! Inside the Amazing Success of Today's Most Popular Chef.* (Hoboken, NJ: John Wiley & Sons, 2004.)
3. Grossman

4. "Get to Know the First Family of New Orleans Cuisine." *Forbes Travel Guide.* September 12, 2013. http://blog.forbestravelguide. com/get-to-know-the-first-family-of-new-orleans-cuisine (accessed June 1, 2015).

5. Turner, Marcia Layton

6. Knapp, Gwendolyn. "Emeril Looks Back on the Restaurant That Started It All." *Eater.com.* March 27, 2015. http://www.eater.com/ 2015/3/27/8297241/emeril-lagasse-new-orleans-emerils-anniversary-NOLA (accessed May 25, 2015).

7. Price, Todd A. "25 years ago, Emeril Lagasse unleashed Emeril's, 'radically altering' Creole cooking." *NOLA.com.* March 12, 2015. http://www.nola.com/dining/index.ssf/2015/03/emeril_lagasse_ new_orleans_eme.html (accessed May 25, 2015).

8. Knapp, Gwendolyn.

9. Price, Todd A.

Chapter 4: **Making It Big in the Big Easy**

1. Schoenfeld, Bruce. "Emeril's Empire." *Cigar Aficionado.* September/October 2005. http://www.cigaraficionado.com/ webfeatures/show/id/Emerils-Empire_6192 (accessed May 25, 2015).

2. Grossman, John. "Recipe for Success." *Cigar Aficionado.* January/ February 1998. http://www.cigaraficionado.com/webfeatures/ show/id/Recipe-for-Success_6067 (accessed June 1, 2015).

3. Akkam, Alia. "The 10 Dishes That Made My Career: Emeril Lagasse." *First We Feast.* September 29, 2014. http://firstwefeast. com/eat/emeril-lagasse-career-changing-dishes/ (accessed June 1, 2015).

4. Knapp, Gwendolyn. "Emeril Looks Back on the Restaurant That Started It All." *Eater.com.* March 27, 2015. http://www.eater. com/2015/3/27/8297241/emeril-lagasse-new-orleans-emer-ils-anniversary-NOLA (accessed May 25, 2015).

5. Sheff, David. "Playboy Interview: Emeril Lagasse." *Playboy.* February 1, 1999. http://business.highbeam.com/137462/article-

1G1-53634808/playboy-interview-emeril-lagasse (accessed May 25, 2015).

6. Price, Todd A. "Emeril's Reviewed in 1990: 'Long May It Live!'" *NOLA.com.* August 10, 1990. http://www.nola.com/dining/index. ssf/1990/08/emerils_reviewed_in_1990_long.html (accessed May 25, 2015).

7. Ruhlman, Michael. *The Reach of a Chef: Professional Cooks in the Age of Celebrity.* (New York: Penguin Books, 2007.)

8. Martin, Chuck. "Emeril Is Elvis of Food." The *Cincinnati Enquirer.* November 21, 1999. http://www.enquirer.com/editions/1999/11/ 21/loc_emeril_is_elvis_of.html (accessed June 1, 2015).

Chapter 5: Bam! Emeril Becomes a Hit

1. Salkin, Allen. *From Scratch: Inside the Food Network.* (New York: G.P. Putnam's Sons, 2013.)

2. "(Cabbage) Heads Will Roll: How To Make A Food Network 'From Scratch'" *NPR.com.* October 13, 2013.

3. Lagasse, Emeril. *Emeril's Delmonico.* (New York: HarperCollins, 2005.)

4. Martin, Chuck. "Emeril Is Elvis of Food." The *Cincinnati Enquirer.* November 21, 1999. http://www.enquirer.com/editions/1999/11/ 21/loc_emeril_is_elvis_of.html (accessed June 22, 2015).

5. Vigue, Doreen Iudica. "Kicking it up a Notch." *Boston Globe.* April 26, 1998.

6. "A Look Back on the History of Emeril Live." Martha Stewart. http://www.marthastewart.com/999683/look-back-history-emeril-live#999683 (accessed June 22, 2015).

7. Hesser, Amanda. "Under the Toque; 'Here's Emeril!' Where's The Chef?" The *New York Times.* November 4, 1998. http:// www.nytimes.com/1998/11/04/dining/under-the-toque-here-s-emeril-where-s-the-chef.html?pagewanted=2 (accessed May 25, 2015).

8. Martin, Chuck. "Emeril Is Elvis of Food." The *Cincinnati Enquirer.* November 21, 1999. http://www.enquirer.com/editions/1999/11/ 21/loc_emeril_is_elvis_of.html (accessed June 22, 2015).

Chapter 6: The Empire Strikes Back

1. "Bernard Carmouche." *Orlando Sentinel.* February 23, 2011. http://articles.orlandosentinel.com/2011-02-23/features/os-chf-carmoche-20110223_1_bernard-carmouche-emeril-s-miami-beach-lookout-for-young-talent (accessed June 22, 2015).
2. Mandell, Andrea. "Emeril Lagasse gets a 'Fresh' start on the Cooking Channel." USAToday. July 3, 2010. http://usatoday30.usa today.com/life/people/2010-07-02-Emeril02_CV_N.htm (accessed June 1, 2015).
3. "Meet Emeril Lagasse's Wife." *Sip & Savor.* November 6, 2013. http://gotidbits.com/new-orleans/the-woman-behind-the-bam#
4. Schoenfeld, Bruce. "Emeril's Empire." *Cigar Aficionado.* September/October 2005. http://www.cigaraficionado.com/webfeatures/show/id/Emerils-Empire_6192 (accessed May 25, 2015).
5. Grossman, John. "Recipe for Success." *Cigar Aficionado.* January/February 1998. http://www.cigaraficionado.com/webfeatures/show/id/Recipe-for-Success_6067 (accessed May 25, 2015).

Chapter 7: End of an Era and New Beginnings

1. Jensen, Elizabeth. "Changing Courses at the Food Network." The *New York Times.* December 17, 2007. http://www.nytimes.com/2007/12/17/business/media/17food.html?pagewanted=print (accessed May 25, 2015).
2. Mandell, Andrea. "Emeril Lagasse gets a 'Fresh' start on the Cooking Channel." *USAToday.* July 3, 2010. http://usatoday30.usa today.com/life/people/2010-07-02-Emeril02_CV_N.htm (accessed June 22, 2015).
3. Wood, Jennifer. "Emeril Lagasse on Opening-Night Disasters, Getting Fired, and 25 Years in the Biz." *Details.com.* March 31, 2015. http://www.details.com/blogs/daily-details/2015/03/emeril-lagasse-on-the-lessons-hes-learned-behind-the-line-and-in-front-of-the-camera.html (accessed May 25, 2015).
4. Ibid.

chicory—A caffeine-free herb thats root is a popular addition to coffee, especially in New Orleans.

confit (con-fee)—something (usually poultry) cooked in its own fat and preserved.

executive chef—Also called chef manager, this is the person in charge of the kitchen in a restaurant.

flan—A sweetened egg custard with a caramel topping.

gluten—Proteins found in wheat and related grains.

gnocchi (no-kee)—Soft, doughy dumplings made from potato.

gumbo—A spicy type stew that originated in southern Louisiana and is served over rice and features okra, seafood, and sausage.

jambalaya—A spicy Louisiana dish of rice cooked with ham, sausage, chicken or shellfish, herbs and spices, as well as tomatoes, onions, celery, and peppers.

jicama (hee-ka-ma)—A Mexican root vegetable that is crisp and juicy like an apple.

line chef—Also called a station chef or *chef de partie,* this person works under the executive chef or sous chef. These chefs are responsible for prepping ingredients and putting together dishes according to restaurant recipes and specifications. Line chefs usually work on specific station, such as the grill, stove or vegetable prep area.

Maître d'—A dining-room attendant who is in charge of the waiters or the entire dining room.

muscadine —A type of grape.

okra—Sometimes called gumbo pods, this vegetable grows in beaked pods and is often used in gumbo.

Pernod—A brand of anise- or licorice-flavored liqueur.

po boy—A traditional sandwich from Louisiana.

remoulade (rom-oo-lawd)—A cold sauce created from a mix of mayonnaise and various condiments and herbs, including pickle relish, capers, mustard, parsley, chervil, and tarragon.

roux (roo)—A mixture of butter or other fat and flour used to thicken sauces and soups.

soufflé—A lightly baked cake made with egg yolks and beaten egg whites, served as a savory or sweet dessert.

sous chef—The chef who is second in command below the executive or head chef.

timbale (tim-baal)—A creamy mixture of meat or vegetables baked in a mold.

FURTHER READING

Books

Locricchio, Matthew. *Teen Cuisine*. Seattle, WA: Skyscape, 2014.

Marchive, Laurane. *The Green Teen Cookbook*. San Francisco, CA: Zest Books, 2014.

Mendocino Press. *The Cookbook for Teens*. Mendocino, California: Mendocino Press, 2014.

Salkin, Allen. *From Scratch: Inside the Food Network*. New York, NY: G.P. Putnam's Sons, 2013.

Websites

Cooking Teens

cookingteens.com

Healthy and tasty recipes for young chefs, as well as articles on young people involved with cooking.

Teen Recipes

teen-recipes.com

A wealth of delicious and simple recipes that teens can prepare.

Movies

Chef. directed by Jon Favreau. 2014.

The Hundred-Foot Journey. by Lasse Hallström. 2014.

INDEX